Praise for *Getting Sober* and Kelly Madigan Erlandson

"*Getting Sober* is a clearly written, no-nonsense guide for anyone who wants to stop drinking. At a time in our culture when the hard-partying ways of 'celebrities' are glamorized by the tabloids, Kelly's book can serve as a helping hand to anyone who wants to get on the road to sobriety. *Getting Sober* answers many questions and concerns one may have about the process and is a powerful tool, available to all, toward a new sober life. I highly recommend this book for anyone who may be curious about getting sober."

—Kristin Davis, star of "Sex and the City"

"A thoughtful and comprehensive guide to those early, crucial days of sobriety. I wish there had been a book like this when I was getting sober. Kelly Madigan Erlandson's book will help many who are beginning their trudge on the road to happy destiny."

—Christopher Kennedy Lawford, author of *Symptoms of Withdrawal: A Memoir of Snapshots and Redemption*

"This book reflects Erlandson's years of professional work with people whose drinking is a problem in their lives. It is honest, direct, comprehensive and practical. Madigan Erlandson speaks to the real questions people have—how to find money for treatment, what happens in AA, and how to deal with cravings. She even covers the resources for sobriety in cyberspace. Her tone is unfailingly kind, understanding, and hopeful. She presents attaining sobriety as a series of steps that anyone can take into a calmer, more creative, stable and joyful future. This book is a unique contribution to literature in the recovery field. I will give it to any of my friends who want to stop drinking."

—Mary Pipher, author of *Reviving Ophelia* and *Writing to Change the World*

"I have been writing and publishing poetry for fifty years and I have yet to offer the public anything as helpful and useful as *Getting Sober*. It is extremely well written, wise, and welcoming."

—Ted Kooser, U.S. Poet Laureate, 2004–2006

"What I found most wonderful about it, besides its simple (though not easy) step-by-step guide to getting sober, was the no-blame, no-shame, nonjudgmental tone. Such a nonthreatening voice will make it possible for anyone struggling with addiction to read it while still maintaining his or her integrity. It is a whole-person approach to addressing alcoholism. Its message will stand the test of time."

—Susan Richards, author of *Chosen by a Horse*

GETTING SOBER

A PRACTICAL GUIDE TO MAKING IT THROUGH THE FIRST 30 DAYS

KELLY MADIGAN ERLANDSON, LADC

New York Chicago San Francisco Lisbon London Madrid Mexico City
Milan New Delhi San Juan Seoul Singapore Sydney Toronto

The McGraw·Hill Companies

Library of Congress Cataloging-in-Publication Data

Erlandson, Kelly Madigan.
Getting sober : a practical guide to making it through the first 30 days / Kelly Madigan Erlandson.
p. cm.
ISBN 978-0-07-149377-2 (alk. paper)
1. Alcoholics—Rehabilitation. I. Title.

HV5275.E75 2008
616.86'103—dc22 2007020138

1 2 3 4 5 6 7 8 9 10 11 12 13 14 15 16 17 18 19 20 21 FGR/FGR 0 9 8 7

Interior design by Monica Baziuk

ISBN 978-0-07-149377-2
MHID 0-07-149377-8

The information contained in this book is intended to provide helpful and informative material on the subject addressed. It is not intended to serve as a replacement for professional medical advice. Any use of the information in this book is at the reader's discretion. The author and publisher specifically disclaim any and all liability arising directly or indirectly from the use or application of any information contained in this book. A health-care professional should be consulted regarding your specific situation.

This book is printed on acid-free paper.

For those who have not yet found their way.

Contents

Acknowledgments ix
Introduction xiii

1 Beginning 1
2 Clearing a Space 9
3 Withdrawal Wake-Up Call 17
4 Making a Decision About Professional Treatment 23
5 What You Need to Know About Alcoholics Anonymous 37
6 Preparing for Sobriety and Dealing with Cravings 51
7 The Banned-from-My-Hand Rule 59
8 Staying Sober Online 65
9 Unexpected and Unmanageable Feelings 73

10 Drinking Triggers 87
11 Staying in Balance Physically 105
12 Healthy Alternatives 111
13 What You Need to Know About Sponsors 125
14 Restoring Your Spirit 137
15 Notes About Failure 145

Afterword: Seeing Beyond Thirty Days 155
Index 169

Acknowledgments

I HAVE been privileged to work with every client who has walked through my office door, and I am grateful for all they have taught and continue to teach me. I have had the opportunity to work side by side with many talented and compassionate colleagues. Of those, the three who stand out as significant mentors and role models are Jody Gilfillan, Duke Engel, and Otto Schultz.

The following people read and commented on various stages of the manuscript, and it improved because of their insightful feedback: Julie Blake Fisher, Eric Erlandson, Jaime Hackbart, Cindy Martin, Roxanna Wood, Jon Brt, Mari Nansel, Marianne Woeppel, Jody Gilfillan, Nicole Church, Amy Plettner, and Otto Schultz. They have each been of assistance in other important ways as well.

Support was also provided by Mary Madigan, Cindy Heider Kaliff, Elizabeth Lowe, Karen Gettert Shoemaker, Mali Fox, Duke Engel, Pam Handy, Virginia Thompson, Paige Namuth, Pam Hasse, Melissa Tubbs Loya, Deb Walz, Lorie Chrastil, Aleta Braun, Ann Chwatsky, Susan Maciaszek, and Amie Bruneau. A crucial moment of hand-holding was provided by Jami Petersen and Brooke Roman.

A substantial portion of this manuscript was completed while I was a writer-in-residence at the Kimmel Harding Nelson Center for the Arts. The gift of uninterrupted time helped immensely. Just prior to the onset of this project, I was a writer-in-residence at Jentel Artist Residency Program, and the time there helped prepare me for this undertaking.

Thank you to Mary Pipher; Christopher Kennedy Lawford; my agent, Sharlene Martin; and my editor, John Aherne. Together they made this possible. Also, I extend my gratitude to Ted Kooser, Kristin Davis, and Susan Richards.

Thank you to my parents, Thomas and Marion Madigan, and to my siblings, Thomas Madigan II and Lori Folts, and to my extended family, all of whom supported and influenced me and participated in a family life in which books were valued.

I am fortunate to have married the smartest man I ever met, Eric Erlandson, and to have the two most amazing daughters on the planet, Tara Polly and Maggie Erlandson. I am also blessed with a remarkable son-in-law, Benjamin Polly. They have been my enthusiastic supporters and my heart's joy.

Finally, this project has been guided and nurtured in ways I cannot begin to view as accidental. For this, thank you, Spirit.

Introduction

ARE YOU ready to quit drinking? If you find yourself with this book in your hands, maybe it's time. You've made promises to yourself or to people you hold dear and have been unable to follow through. You have alternately worried about your drinking and tried to dismiss it as no big deal, though deep down inside you knew better. There may have been times when your drinking has humiliated you by causing problems with your job, the law, or your family. You may have done things you don't think you can ever forgive yourself for. Attempts to quit drinking entirely may have lasted a few weeks, a couple of months, or maybe only a day or two.

You might be ashamed of yourself for not being able to get a handle on this and have probably wondered what exactly is wrong with you. Why do others seem to be able to drink without experiencing the difficulties that you do? Maybe you have tried different approaches to solve the problem, such as limiting yourself to a certain number of drinks, only taking a set amount of money with you to the bar, switching from hard liquor to beer, or only allowing yourself to drink on special occasions. When these techniques eventually failed, you may have tried only drinking on weekends, not allowing yourself to drink before (or after) a certain time of day, or avoiding a particular type of alcohol—tequila, for instance—that always gets you in trouble. Maybe you've prayed for a solution.

The truth is, once you have crossed a certain line in your relationship with alcohol, cutting back won't work for you. You may be able to hold it together for a while, but eventually the drinking gets out of hand again and bad things start to happen. You have a moment of clarity in which you can see that your drinking is a problem, you renew your efforts to control it, and you find yourself surprised to end up right back where you started—in trouble with your drinking.

Maybe you didn't choose this book for yourself. It may have been handed to you by a physician who is concerned about the effects of alcohol on your health, or assigned to you by a judge or probation officer after a DWI conviction. It could be part of a packet of materials given to you in an alcohol treatment facility, where you have been sent by your family or by the court. Maybe you are reading this in jail or in the hospital.

Whether you picked it up yourself or had it handed to you by someone else, the message is the same. No matter how many months or years you have struggled with this issue, no matter how bad your current situation may seem, no matter how many times you have tried before and failed, there is hope for you. You can learn how to quit drinking and also be happy, which may look impossible to you today. The damage you have done to yourself and to your life can be repaired. Your spirit can be restored. You can feel proud of yourself again. The steps you will need to take in order to accomplish this will not be easy, but they will be very clear.

I don't believe there is one solution that works for everyone. However, since 1983, I have been counseling people on the threshold of sobriety, and I have observed as many failed and many succeeded. I've noticed that those who succeed share a common set of tools that they employ to find their way to a fulfilling new way of life. You could continue to try to figure this problem out on your own, or you could learn from the collective wisdom and ingenuity of those who have gone before you. There are no guarantees, but if you are serious about quitting, taking the practical steps spelled out in this book will give you a very good chance of achieving your goal.

Every day when I show up for work at the treatment center, I feel privileged to be there. People have asked me how I can do such a depressing job, and I tell them they have it all wrong—working at a treatment center is like working at a miracle factory, a place where people with broken spirits repair themselves. I hope to share some of that restoration with you, in the hope that it can help you find your way.

The question is, are you ready? Are you prepared to face the issue directly, to stop trying to avoid admitting what you already know is true about yourself? Are you ready to let go of your methods of cutting down, which never worked in the long run anyway? Are you willing to wave the white flag, accept some help, and start moving forward? If so, your life will begin to change rapidly. Your head will begin to clear, your body will begin the process of healing itself, and you will find ways to be sober without being miserable.

Maybe you aren't completely certain you are ready to quit. You may still believe that under the right circumstances, you could cut back enough to get on with your life. Let's take a closer look at that idea. Get out a piece of paper and a pen. At the top, write "Ways I Have Tried to Quit or Control My Drinking in the Past." Now, being completely honest with yourself, list every method you have ever tried, no matter how absurd it may seem to you today. List the plan you had to drink only on certain days of the week or only between certain hours, to buy smaller bottles, or to time your drinks. Think back to times you intentionally arrived at a function late so that you wouldn't be too drunk by the end of it. Maybe you moved away so you wouldn't be influenced by your surroundings or your drinking friends, or you signed up for a gym membership so you could counter the negative health effects the alcohol was having on your body. Did you vow to never drink on an empty stomach again? Maybe you quit drinking for Lent, or as a New Year's resolution, or as a promise to your spouse or children.

Now take a long look at that list. Some of those measures may have worked for a while, and the others failed almost immediately. The truth is, if you could manage your drinking, you would have. If you could successfully quit drinking on your own, common sense says you would have done so a long time ago. This does not mean that you are a worthless failure with no willpower. It means that you, like millions of others, have a drinking problem that you can't solve on your own. This problem does not respond to willpower, good intentions, or promises. You cannot simply pledge to be different.

Maybe your drinking has taken you so far down that you wonder if you are a hopeless case and question whether it is even worth trying. Please remember that people older than you, people younger than you, people who have tried and failed more times than you have, people on a waiting list for a liver transplant, people with an alcohol-related criminal record twenty pages long, and people who were quietly drinking their lives away have all managed to find their way into sobriety eventually. While you're alive, there is no reason to ever give up hope.

If you want to learn how to cut back or drink moderately, if you think you may still be able to wrestle this problem without quitting entirely, this is not the book for you. There are no clues here for drinking less, no tips for hiding your drinking from your employer, no concoctions that cure hangovers. However, if you find that you are ready to get completely sober, there are answers for you in these pages.

One more thing, before we get started. Although you may be ashamed of your issues with alcohol, and the behavior that went along with it, getting sober is not a shameful undertaking. It is one of the most honorable things you will ever do. It is the doorway to remembering who you really are, reclaiming your self-respect, pursuing lost dreams, and feeling a sense of meaning and purpose in your life. The pain, embarrassment, and humiliation you may be feeling right now have brought you to the threshold. Are you ready?

1

Beginning

If you have already quit drinking, and it has been less than one week since you quit, please jump ahead to Chapter 3 and read "Withdrawal Wake-Up Call." Afterward, you can return to this page and continue reading. If you have not yet quit drinking, you can do a few things to get ready before you actually quit. Let's get right to it.

Gathering Supplies

You will need to gather some supplies to begin your journey toward sobriety. It will be helpful to have:

- A couple of good pens
- A notebook or blank journal

- Bottled water in single-serving sizes
- A library card
- A membership card to a movie-rental business
- A three-by-five-inch index card
- A phone book

If you are in a situation where you cannot get these things together, one pen or pencil and some paper will suffice.

You're Going to Have to Get Some Help

The paradox of getting and staying sober is that although it is one of the most personal things you will do in your lifetime, it is something you cannot do alone. This may be the single most difficult truth about sobriety. You may have strong feelings regarding this. Many people insist that their drinking problem is their problem, not anyone else's, and they intend to solve it themselves. For some, this type of independence is something they strongly value.

You may also feel overwhelmed with shame because of your drinking problem. It was hard enough to admit it to yourself, and you don't relish the thought of admitting it to others. You may fear that others will see you as weak-willed, ineffective, or pathetic. In reality, getting sober is a respectable activity. It signals your desire to clean up whatever mess you may have made and take responsibility for your life.

We have all been flooded with cultural messages, such as "if you want something done right, do it yourself," that suggest relying on others is some sort of weakness. This narrow view does not account for the many things we cannot do alone. Cooperation among groups of people allows us to achieve far beyond what one individual can do in a lifetime. And some things simply cannot be done at all unless people work together toward a common goal. Sobriety is one of those things. It requires the support and cooperation of others in order to flourish.

Although you may have pushed some people away with your drinking behavior, it is probable that there are some people who care about you and would still be willing to help you if you'd be willing to let them. If you have living parents, siblings, or children, they are the most likely candidates. Sometimes a key support person might be a coworker or a minister. It is possible you may have a close friend, or more than one friend, who could help you as well. But let's take a look at that friend situation before you decide for sure.

The Drinking Buddy

Some people with drinking problems drink alone, and others drink with friends. If you have done much of your drinking with others, you may have developed a special kind of friend called a "drinking buddy." These friendships are marked by their camaraderie, their sense of mutual support, and the common activity of drinking together. Because your drinking buddies may have their own issues with alcohol, they can't be relied on to help you get sober.

It is difficult to distinguish a drinking buddy from a true friend while you are still drinking—you all laugh at the same jokes, drink at the same pace, and have a great time together. Once you stop drinking for a while, however, the jokes won't seem so funny anymore, and staying out until 4:00 A.M. watching your "friends" drink and get drunk, while you sip seltzer water, would become very old, very fast. Because of the difficulty of telling your friends and your drinking buddies apart in the early days of sobriety, you shouldn't consider any of your friends to be key support people for getting sober unless they are friends you do not drink with, ever. Later, you may discover some of the friends whom you have drunk with can be counted on to support you. In the beginning, however, it is best to rely on the friends you have who don't drink and family members or other concerned people who are not a part of your drinking life.

Support List

You have your supplies, right? It is time to make another list. Write down the names of all the people you can think of who might support your decision to get sober. Include them on the list even if you haven't talked to them in some time. Don't put anyone on the list who might even come close to meeting the definition of a drinking buddy. Later, we'll take another look at those friendships to see whether we can decide which ones are true friends. But for now, leave them off the list.

If you can't think of even one person to put on your list, think again. It is rare that a person has cut ties with every other human being in his or her life. Think about people in your family who may be mad or angry or disappointed in you now but who would rally to your aid in this time of need. Consider previous employers, friends from school, cousins, or your neighbor. In rare situations, people have listed their attorney, their probation officer, a caseworker, or their judge.

Think of anyone who may have offered to help you in the past or expressed concern. Keep in mind that you won't be asking people on this support list to donate an organ for you. This is just a list of people you can trust to lend a helping hand and to help out in a small way during this time in your life. Surely there is *someone* who hasn't completely given up on you.

One danger to be aware of is the possibility that you may have included someone on the list who should not have been listed. Let's say you have a relationship that recently ended. Maybe it wasn't your decision to end the relationship, and you'd like to get back together. You suspect, or maybe you flat-out know, that your drinking was part of the problem in the relationship. If you call this person now and ask for his or her support as you quit drinking, you may be viewed as insincere. It could be seen as manipulative on your part. It would be best to steer clear of these confusing interactions. Leave that person out of the sobriety plan, for now.

If you are still unable to list even one person, you will need to pay very close attention to the section in this book about Alcoholics Anonymous. There you will find people who care about your effort to get sober even though they have never met you.

Hopefully you now have a list of people who you believe would be willing to support your decision to quit drinking. It may be a short list, maybe only one or two names, or it may be a long list. Next, write down the phone number and e-mail address of each person on your support list. If you have lost touch with someone, look up the number or call someone else who can give you the number. If you cannot get a current phone number for the person, write down his or her mailing address.

Enlisting Support

Now that you have a list of people who might be willing to support you, the next step is enlisting their support.

You may be reluctant to contact them because of the things you said or did to them while you were drinking. You may feel ashamed or embarrassed about calling them, or you might not want to burden them with your problem. You might worry that they will be tired of hearing your empty promises about how you are going to quit. These are common feelings, but the truth is you are going to need some help from other people in order to succeed with your plan to get sober. Consider calling them even if it makes you uncomfortable.

Start by choosing a person from your support list whom you think you would able to talk to about what you are doing and give that person a call. Make the first call an "easy" one. Tell him or her that you realize you need to quit drinking and that you want to do so. Do not promise anything. Explain that you are willing to do whatever you can to get sober and that you will need some support and help. Say that you do not know exactly what you will need from him or her, but ask if it would be OK to call with requests for help related to getting sober. Almost certainly, the person on your list will agree to help you. And if he or she doesn't, simply accept the fact that this person is not in a position to help you at the moment, for whatever reason, and move on to the next person on the list. Do not use these phone calls as an attempt to clear things up or to apologize profusely. Simply ask for help.

After you have done this with one person from your list, you might not feel as resistant to calling others. It would be best to call each person on your list and have that same conversation that you had with the first person. If you have a long support list, don't expect yourself to get this done in one day. Spread it out over several days. If calling them all seems unrealistic, or too overwhelming to you, choose at least three people from your list and make a commitment to contact them over the next three days. You might tell yourself that calling one person is enough in your case because of how loyal or helpful that one person is likely to be. Unfortunately, it is not good to rely solely on one person. That person may have other commitments, including a job, travel, or family obligations. Your support person could also come down with the flu or be asleep or unavailable when you need something. Don't shortchange yourself at this early point in the planning. Talk to at least three people about your need for their support.

2

Clearing a Space

DEDICATED DRINKING consumes a great deal of space in one's life. It is often where your thoughts are likely to dwell. You might spend time thinking about drinking; or worrying about whether your current supply is adequate, trying to remember when the liquor store closes or if it's going to be open on Sunday; or regretting your inability to quit when you have tried. You might also spend time and effort hiding your drinking, or the effects of your drinking, from those around you. You may have spent time devising ingenious hiding places for your alcohol, creating excuses for why you've missed work or important family functions, or concocting hangover cures. You have certainly spent time recovering from the physical consequences of consuming too much alcohol.

You've probably also collected a variety of alcohol-related memorabilia over the years, such as a beer can collection, a wine decanter display, or lighted neon beer signs. You may have attire, such as a T-shirt, tie, or ball cap, that advertises your favorite brand of alcohol or references drinking. You may have acquired special coolers, ice-cube trays, keg equipment, corkscrews, or martini glasses. These items take up physical space, but they also stake a claim on your personal identity, reminding you of your life of drinking. Setting these items aside as you clear space for your sobriety may be harder than it first appears. You likely have some attachment to these items, either because they remind you of drinking or because they are mementos of a good friend or a fun time you once had. You may not be ready to let go of them all, and that will not be required. However, it will be important that you remove yourself from the influence of these items.

Clearing the Physical Space

Contact one of the people on your support list and ask if he or she has an hour to help you with a project related to your sobriety. Ask the person to come over and to bring some boxes along. Together, the two of you can gather up all of your alcohol-related items. Be sure to include any favorite drinking glasses or beer mugs. Go through your closets and remove the T-shirts, boxer shorts, hats, ties, and sweatshirts that have alcohol-related logos or sayings. Throw away any of these items that you are ready to release. The remainder of the items should be packed into boxes. Ask your support person if he or she would be willing to store them for you for a month or two. If not, ask someone else from your list to store them. If you have no one on your list, or none of those people can store the items, pack those boxes in a remote place such as the rafters of the garage, a corner of the basement, or the back of a closet.

You will also need to locate any supplies of alcohol that you may still have, including beer in the refrigerator, a supply of alcohol in the garage, and hidden bottles you have stashed around the house, in your vehicle, outside in the shed, or at your workplace. Try not to overlook any possible hiding place where you may have alcohol stored. You should not do this search by yourself. Take your support person with you. While you have permission to store some of your favorite memorabilia that you cannot yet part with in your house if there is nowhere else for you to store it, this is not the case with the alcohol itself. It has to go, and it should go right away, with no exceptions. With your support person, pour it out or have him or her take it away. You will sabotage your sobriety if you try to get sober while living in a home where alcohol also resides.

Special Cases

Some of you may be arguing that you have a special case. Wine collectors have said their collection is an investment, and they never drink that wine anyway, so it should be allowed to stay. Plus, the collection is too big to store at someone else's house, and it needs to be kept at a certain temperature in a wine cellar. Others have argued that they still want to be able to offer a beer or a drink to their friends when they come over, or that they live with someone who does not have a drinking problem but who enjoys having a beer after work or a glass of wine with dinner. The argument goes that the person living with me shouldn't have to suffer because of my problem. Let's examine those "special cases."

The Expensive Collection. If you absolutely refuse to part with an expensive wine, whiskey, or tequila collection, look for any opportunity to store it elsewhere. Consider renting a storage unit. Ask to store it at a friend's place who might have more room. Better yet, give some more thought to getting rid of it altogether. Having your identity tied to an alcohol collection is not going to serve you well as you try to create your new lifestyle. If you've been saving these bottles of alcohol as an investment, sell them now and buy some other investment like a mutual fund or gold coins. Get that collection out of your possession, out of your home, and hopefully out of your mind.

The Friends Who Stop Over. What about serving a beer to a friend who stops over? This is not a good idea. In fact, it is a setup for failure for your sobriety. To be prepared to serve beer, wine, or mixed drinks to friends, you would have to store those items in your home, and this is one of the fastest routes to disaster. For the time being, even if it feels like you are being rude or a poor host, don't serve alcohol in your home. Offer a friend a soft drink, a smoothie, water, or iced tea—while a drinking buddy might scoff at the notion, a true friend will understand your situation and be more than happy to take whatever you have to offer. Simply put: do not keep alcohol in your house for friends.

Living with Someone Who Drinks. It is likely that the people living with you have already suffered because of your problem. They have suffered inconvenience, concern, emotional distress, or just plain old-fashioned aggravation because of your drinking. They are likely to be willing to support your decision to make life easier for you and themselves, and if in fact they do not have a drinking problem of their own, getting all of the alcohol out of the house so that you can pursue this important goal will not be an issue. They are still free to go to a bar or restaurant or to a friend's house for an occasional drink if they are in the mood—which would be a small price to pay for a more stable living situation. If, however, they feel the need to have alcohol in the house for whatever reason, ask them to keep it in their own personal space.

What if you do live with a person who has a drinking issue of his or her own? If you live with people who are dedicated drinkers like yourself, you are in an unsafe recovery environment. This means that right where you live, you will run up against situations that will make your goal of sobriety much more difficult to obtain. This troublesome issue is not easily solved.

You could approach the people you live with and ask them to support your goal of sobriety. Ask them if they are willing to clear the alcohol out of the house and not drink in front of you or leave any alcohol, including empty bottles, where you would see it. Even if they agree, you need to face the truth that they may not follow through with this agreement. As you yourself may no doubt be aware, sometimes dedicated drinkers forget the agreements they have made or cannot adhere to them. Be prepared, at any time, to run across alcohol that has been left in plain view by your housemates. Pay special attention to the section in Chapter 7 titled "The Banned-from-My-Hand Rule."

If you do live with dedicated drinkers you will need to strongly consider living somewhere else during your first thirty days of sobriety. Carefully read the section in Chapter 4 about treatment options. If treatment is unavailable to you, think about living temporarily with a person on your support list. Your dangerous recovery environment is one of the hardest barriers to overcome as you get sober. Drinking has a contagious quality that makes it especially difficult to abstain when your friends or family are in the house drinking. Do whatever you can to avoid this situation.

Where You Like to Drink

Next, let's take a look at your favorite place in the house to drink. Maybe you sit in the kitchen with a drink in one hand and a cigarette in the other. Perhaps it is a favorite recliner while you watch TV. Maybe you have a special relaxing spot set up for yourself in the garage, away from the noise of the rest of the house. Maybe you drink in your own bedroom. Whatever room it is, it is time for a change.

This is another opportunity for a person from your support list to help you. Clean this room, get rid of any old junk you may have stored here, and rearrange the furniture.

Throw a bright blanket or sheet over your favorite chair. Move things enough to really alter the look and feel of the room. Clean the room very well, checking under the furniture for any empties or hidden supplies of alcohol. Dust, scrub, vacuum, wash walls, and haul trash out. You are dedicating this room, this space, for new and better uses. With the alcohol gone, any memorabilia or supplies packed up and shipped out, and your favorite drinking place reordered, you now have some room in your life for sobriety.

3

Withdrawal Wake-Up Call

WHATEVER YOU do, don't skip this section. It is imperative that you understand that withdrawal from alcohol can be life-threatening and will require medical assessment to get through safely.

What Is Withdrawal?

Your alcohol use is far more than a bad habit or a mental obsession. Over time, you have taught your body to expect and prepare for the regular ingestion of this substance. Because the body works hard to stay in balance, it makes changes based on your regular habits. You have conditioned your body to be ready at all times to process alcohol. Unfortunately, your body doesn't make changes as fast as your mind does. If you stop drinking suddenly, which you are about to do, your body cannot adapt quickly. It is still expecting the alcohol.

Your body has prepared for the alcohol by speeding up the central nervous system. This has been a self-preservation technique on its part, since the alcohol you have been consuming is a central nervous system depressant, meaning it slows down some basic functions, like breathing and heart rate. Because your body wants to perform at optimum speed, it has adjusted to this regular alcohol consumption by speeding up some of these natural functions. It speeds them up, the alcohol slows them down, and your body achieves something like a normal rate of functioning, at least where breathing and heart rate are concerned. The long-term effects of this are detrimental and may include high blood pressure or renal failure, but in the short term, it is the body's attempt to be efficient.

Withdrawal is what can happen when you suddenly stop drinking. The body is still geared up for the regular dose, and it takes your body about two to five days to figure out the alcohol isn't coming and to adjust to its absence. It can take even longer if your alcohol use has been very long term or in very large quantities.

Withdrawal Can Be Life-Threatening

Many people have the mistaken belief that withdrawal is simply a period of discomfort, during which a person might feel nauseated, shaky, or sweaty. It is much more than that. Alcohol withdrawal is a potentially life-threatening medical condition. In fact, it is one of the most dangerous substances to withdraw from—much more dangerous than withdrawal from methamphetamine or cocaine, for example. It lasts only a few days, maybe a week to ten days at the longest, but it is a very serious medical situation that you need to know more about before you quit drinking.

Because the central nervous system has been trained to operate at an abnormally fast pace to counteract the alcohol, when the alcohol is no longer present to balance that out, people experience a variety of symptoms as they go through withdrawal. These include but are not limited to shakiness, headaches, difficulty sleeping, excessive sweating, confusion, hallucinations (both visual and auditory), anxiety, nausea, increased blood pressure, and seizures. Withdrawal symptoms need to be taken seriously.

Medical Assistance for Withdrawal Symptoms

The risk of seizure and other serious symptoms of alcohol withdrawal can be well managed with medication such as benzodiazepines. To obtain this medicine, and to have expert supervision of your withdrawal symptoms, you will need medical assistance.

There are a variety of ways for you to obtain the medical help that you need. If you have a physician, before you stop drinking, schedule an appointment and discuss this issue with him or her and explore your options. Be forthright about the amount you drink and the frequency of your alcohol use. Explain that you intend to quit drinking, and ask for his or her guidance. Your doctor may have a plan to help you through the initial days of sobriety, when you are most likely to experience withdrawal symptoms.

If you don't have a doctor, you have other ways to obtain the medical supervision you need. Admit yourself to a freestanding detoxification center, a hospital, or an alcohol treatment center that has a medical or "detox" unit. These organizations are highly skilled at assisting you as you go through withdrawal. They will medically supervise you, watch all of your vital signs carefully, administer any necessary medication to control the symptoms, and help to ensure your safety.

If you opt out of these choices and you begin to experience any physical discomfort from withdrawal, please go to a hospital emergency room immediately. Be warned, though, that seizures—which some people die from—have happened to people who were not aware of any other symptoms. That is, even if you experience no other symptoms of withdrawal, you could still experience a seizure. This is rare, but it can happen. Let a medical professional decide if you are in need of services. Don't take a chance. Do not try to "ride out" alcohol withdrawal on your own.

If the prospect of saving your life isn't enough motivation, medical management of your withdrawal will also make you much more comfortable physically. Many people who have tried to quit on their own in the past found they simply could not tolerate the withdrawal and drank to ease those symptoms. It was as though their minds and bodies were at odds with each other. Some felt like failures and described themselves as lacking willpower. Instead, this is one time when they may have actually saved their own lives by drinking and staving off a potentially fatal reaction to alcohol withdrawal. Medical management of withdrawal can greatly reduce the discomfort, reduce cravings, and allow you to get safely through the dangerous first few days of abstinence.

Please, seek medical help for this early portion of your sobriety. It can prevent serious consequences and will make you much more comfortable during those first few days. If you end up in a situation in which circumstances force you to suddenly stop drinking, such as being hospitalized or jailed, be sure to let the staff know that you may be at risk for withdrawal so they can ensure your safety.

Sometimes people who don't experience any physical withdrawal symptoms will interpret that to mean they don't have a problem after all or that their problem isn't that bad. Don't make this mistake. Genetics, body chemistry, gender, frequency of drinking, and tolerance can all be factors in whether or not you experience physical withdrawal. Just as some people who have only been drinking for a few years can suffer severe withdrawal symptoms, many who have had serious drinking problems quit without noting any physical effects. Even if your body doesn't experience withdrawal symptoms, you could still have a serious drinking problem. Keep in mind that the body's reaction to alcohol is just one part of the larger picture—you have to consider all the other areas of your life where your drinking may have caused damage.

Detoxification services, as we have just discussed, deal with the physical, medical aspects of quitting. There is much more to getting sober than that, however, so let's take a look at your professional treatment options, following your successful withdrawal.

4

Making a Decision About Professional Treatment

As we've seen, getting through the immediate discomfort and danger of alcohol withdrawal symptoms requires medical supervision. But even after the physical symptoms have passed, there are many benefits to getting longer term professional help. Let's examine what that might look like.

Myths and Misconceptions About Professional Treatment

Before you rule out the possibility of getting some professional support while you get sober, let's make sure

Treatment Terminology

Detox: Short for *detoxification*, detox refers to medical services in the first two to five days of abstinence, when you may experience physical discomfort and symptoms that require medical supervision. Detox can be done in a hospital, a freestanding detox unit, or a special unit within an alcohol treatment facility. It could last as long as seven to ten days, if your drinking was very heavy and your symptoms are slow to abate. It does not necessarily include any personal counseling.

Treatment: Treatment usually refers to a combination of group therapy, individual counseling sessions, family involvement, educational components, and peer group support. It can be packaged in several ways.

Rehab: Short for *rehabilitation*, rehab could refer to detoxification, treatment services, or a combination of the two.

Inpatient: Short for *inpatient treatment*, this term refers to the type of program that requires clients to stay overnight in a facility. The more accurate term for this is *residential*, since inpatient, in the insurance world, refers to hospitalization.

you have good information. There are many myths and misperceptions about what treatment is, how it works, and what goes on in "rehab." Dedicated drinkers are often afraid to get treatment services because of these misperceptions. That is unfortunate, because availing yourself of professional help can really accelerate you toward your goal of sobriety.

Professional alcohol counselors can guide you, point out areas where you may need assistance, provide targeted education, and help you make decisions that will enhance your recovery. Basically, they can smooth the road for you. As part of your treatment, you would be educated about alcoholism and various aspects of recovery. You would begin to build a support system by meeting others who are also quitting and by participating in group therapy. You would work with a counselor individually to determine what barriers or issues you most need help with, and a plan would be developed to address those issues. You would be involved in developing the plan.

Treatment Options

Alcohol treatment comes in a variety of packages. Historically, people "checked in" for a "thirty-day stay" at a treatment center. This is not often the case anymore. Treatment used to come in just that one size, but people's needs are all different, and it didn't always fit everyone. Often, people are able to receive counseling services without ever staying overnight at a facility. Sometimes a person's insurance company may want to have a say in selecting the level of care and may only be willing to authorize payment for certain services. See more about this later in this chapter.

Different Levels of Outpatient

The leading edge of treatment, and the type that is most common now, is offered on an outpatient basis.

Outpatient Treatment. In outpatient treatment, you don't spend the night at a treatment center, but you show up for your services and return home. If you have a job, you are often able to continue working. This kind of treatment attempts to work itself around the important parts of your schedule, instead of the other way around. Outpatient treatment comes in a variety of forms, such as meeting with a counselor once a week for an hour or attending a group led by a trained counselor once a week. This is what is usually considered the "outpatient" level of care.

Intensive Outpatient. Treatment is also offered in a package that is referred to as "intensive outpatient." This involves services three or four days per week, usually for about three hours at a time. For instance, you might go to intensive outpatient treatment three evenings a week, from 6:00 until 9:00. Or it could be offered three mornings a week, from 9:00 to 12:00.

Partial Care. For some, three evenings (or mornings) per week is not enough support. The next step up from that is called "partial care." It generally involves six hours a day of services, four or five days per week. Like the other levels of outpatient care, it involves individual work with a counselor, education about alcoholism and recovery, and group sessions with others who are in your same boat—it is just a more sustained and intensive schedule.

Residential Treatment

Some people cannot maintain abstinence from alcohol even with the help of these kinds of outpatient treatment services. Their drinking habits are so well established, their recovery environment is unsupportive, or they simply cannot deal with the cravings. For them, residential treatment is the best option. This involves actually checking in to a treatment center—which can be anything from a wing in the local hospital to a facility located in a quiet, natural setting—for a period of time so that they have support twenty-four hours a day.

Most people who enter residential treatment are fearful to do so and resist it, but once they get to the treatment facility and meet the other clients, they experience some welcomed relief. They often say that treatment is a much better experience than they expected. They describe it as a safe place and are sometimes reluctant to leave when it is completed. They form lasting bonds with the other clients and feel validated and supported. Most of all, they do not feel judged.

Treatment staff understand that alcoholism is not a moral weakness, and typically they have very nurturing and accepting attitudes toward a person with a drinking problem. The residents share similar problems and therefore are able to form connections with each other quickly.

People often fear that residential treatment will mean they are locked up and cannot choose to leave the facility. This is not the case. Unless you are already incarcerated and considering a treatment program within your prison system, you are not likely to find an alcohol treatment center that restricts you from leaving. Alcohol treatment does not involve "quiet rooms" or seclusion. Agreeing to get treatment does not mean that you lose any of your civil rights. If you decide to leave, you are free to leave.

The only exception to this would involve alcohol treatment that takes place as part of a psychiatric facility. Psychiatric facilities can and do restrict people from leaving, but even then it is only if that person has been determined to be a danger to himself or herself or to someone else. This doesn't include some sort of vague, possible future danger, like you are going to drink yourself to death over time. Instead, this refers to people who are actively suicidal today or are making specific threats to harm or kill someone else.

If you are considering a residential treatment facility and you have fears that you could get locked up there, call and ask them about their policies. Ask them to explain to you under what circumstances a client would be prevented from leaving the building. Find out whether there are any exceptions to the policy. You have a right to have this fear addressed before you ever set foot in the place.

You may also have fears about treatment being too confrontational. You may have heard stories or seen movies that involve clients being yelled at, ridiculed, and humiliated in the name of therapy. Alcohol treatment has made significant progress in terms of technique and approach, and few, if any, reputable treatment centers use these techniques. Preserving the dignity of clients should always be one of the foremost goals of the program, and you have the right to ask about this before you start treatment.

This does not mean that alcohol counseling professionals will coddle you or help you maintain false beliefs about yourself. They are likely to be forthright and direct with you to help you address behaviors and attitudes that contribute to your drinking, but they should do so respectfully. The goals of treatment are to help you see yourself more honestly and realistically and to help you acquire the tools you need for sobriety. This may include giving you feedback that is uncomfortable for you to hear and asking you to look at areas of your life that you would rather ignore. Treatment should never involve yelling at you.

If you can approach treatment with an open attitude, the progress you can achieve there is almost unbelievable. You can gain self-respect, a connection with others, and the essential tools of recovery in a short period of time. You will have a place to talk about what you are going through as you navigate the early days and weeks of sobriety. The support of professionals can ease your way considerably as you begin to make these monumental changes in your life.

How Do I Know Which Type of Treatment Is for Me?

To choose the most appropriate level of care for yourself, you will need to get an evaluation, or initial assessment, of your problem. This involves sitting down with a licensed or certified alcohol counselor and reviewing your situation in detail. As part of the assessment process the counselor may administer a written test to you. After the information has been gathered, the counselor will discuss a recommendation with you and provide information to you about where you can receive the services he or she is recommending. Many alcohol treatment centers conduct their own evaluations of new clients, but if the one you contact doesn't do so, they should be able to refer you to someone for a professional evaluation.

The Financial Cost of Treatment

Many fear treatment for another reason altogether: the cost. Treatment services can be expensive, which can be a substantial obstacle for many people who might otherwise benefit from them. There are several ways to overcome this financial hurdle.

If you have health insurance, you may discover that a large portion of the cost of treatment is covered by your insurance plan, especially if you use a treatment provider that is on your plan's approved list. Without a doubt, if you have health insurance your first step toward seeking treatment is to call the number on your insurance card and ask which of your local treatment providers are "approved providers" or "in your network." If you find that you do have coverage, start your treatment search by contacting the treatment programs that are approved by your insurance plan.

The following are some questions to ask your insurance company:

- What percentage of treatment would be paid for by your insurance company?
- Will there be any deductibles or copays?
- What are the limits to the plan's coverage?
- Will your employer or supervisor be able to find out the reason this coverage is necessary?

Some financial questions to ask the treatment centers to include:

- Will you have to pay your portion up front, or will you be billed?
- Is a down payment required?
- Will they bill your insurance plan for you, or will you have to submit the claims yourself?

After asking these questions, you should have a much better idea of where you stand regarding the cost of treatment. You will know which agencies are covered by your plan and what the cost of treatment is for each of those places. Likely you have discovered that part of the cost of treatment will be your responsibility but that a significant portion will be paid by your insurance.

Low-Cost or No-Cost Treatment Centers

Unfortunately, many people do not have medical insurance or have limited plans that do not cover alcohol treatment. If you are one of these people, you still may be able to access treatment services. The federal government, and many state and county governments, provide funding so that uninsured people can get help for their alcohol problems.

How you access these funded programs depends on where you are living. Some of the programs offer services based on a sliding fee scale, which uses your income as a gauge for determining how much to charge you. Other places may require that you meet eligibility for Medicaid to waive the cost of services. Some states have established an agency that authorizes free or reduced-cost treatment through an interview process or a formal application.

In the United States, you can usually locate a local phone number for a free referral service that will assist you in finding affordable treatment services. This is where your phone book, gathered as part of your supplies, can first be used. You may have to search through the phone book, looking for human services agencies, drug crisis lines, or a statewide Council on Alcoholism.

Where these services are listed will vary from state to state, but often they are listed in a separate section of the telephone book. Many other countries around the world have similar listings in their phone books as well.

If you are having trouble finding one of these services, look up the number to a local treatment center, probably listed under "Alcohol" in the directory, and call to ask them for advice. If they cannot assist you themselves, they will likely be able to give you some helpful phone numbers.

If you have access to the Internet—and many public libraries offer Internet access at no cost—you should be able to find a treatment program near you that offers financial assistance. In the United States, for example, you can search through a website hosted by the Substance Abuse & Mental Health Services Administration (SAMHSA), which is part of the United States Department of Health and Human Services. You can find information at http://dasis3.samhsa.gov. The website offers a Substance Abuse Treatment Facility Locator that can be accessed by clicking on your home state. When given the opportunity to "customize" your search, do so. This will allow you to search for specific types of programs in your area, including those with payment assistance.

In Scotland, you can access a list of local services through knowthescore.info, and in England and Wales, drugs.gov.uk/dat/directory is a good starting place. For information about services in Australia, try starting at adin.com.au.

In other countries, type "alcohol treatment" and the name of your country in a search engine to find information on the Internet that may help you access services.

Once you have located the free or low-cost treatment programs in your area, you can begin to call those agencies and ask questions about their programs. Pay close attention to whether they have a waiting list to get into treatment. Many of the funded programs have more requests for help than they can serve in a timely fashion. Find out how long the wait is expected to be and what your options are in the meantime.

If there is a waiting list and you can place yourself on it, consider doing so. You might eventually decide against getting professional help, and if so you can always remove your name from the waiting list. In the meantime, you may have experiences that convince you that you would fare better with some professional help, and if that turns out to be the case, you will have already moved up on the waiting list and will be closer to obtaining that help.

When All Else Fails

What if you don't have insurance that will help you pay for treatment and you cannot access these low-cost services either because they are not available in your area or because you do not meet their eligibility guidelines? In that case, you may still have the option of making a reasonable down payment at a treatment center and making a commitment to pay the rest of the treatment cost through a payment plan. One of the people on your support list may be willing to help you with the down payment if you don't have it yourself.

Realistically, even if you have exhausted all of these possibilities, you may find yourself unable to find treatment that you can afford or that is available when you need it. Luckily, there is a safety net in place—Alcoholics Anonymous.

5

What You Need to Know About Alcoholics Anonymous

ALCOHOLICS ANONYMOUS (AA) is a group of people who come together to help each other solve their common problem. It does not cost money, is run by its own members and not by professionals, and is available almost everywhere. Millions of people from all different backgrounds from all over the world have found AA to be the answer to their drinking problem.

But Alcoholics Anonymous Isn't for Me!

Many people who are struggling to quit drinking feel reluctant to attend AA, in spite of how available and successful it is. People give many different reasons for not wanting to go to AA when they are trying to get sober. Let's examine some of them.

I'm Embarrassed to Go; Someone I Know Might See Me There

You are certainly at risk of being seen and recognized by someone you know at an AA meeting. Consider the possibility that people who know you might already have a clue that you have a drinking problem. Even if you haven't done some act that brought the attention of the media to you, those around you have seen the signs and have come to their own conclusions about you. You likely have a reputation as a heavy drinker or at least have raised people's suspicions. Therefore, they won't be shocked to see you there. Another important factor that people who are getting sober seem to overlook is that if people see you at an AA meeting, it is because they are at an AA meeting. The likelihood that they would judge you for going to the same meeting they are attending is pretty remote. There is nothing shameful about trying to solve your problem. It is your out-of-control drinking, and the behavior that came along with it, that was embarrassing. Getting sober is an honorable activity.

I Don't Believe in God; AA Will Try to Shove Religion Down My Throat

At first glance, AA can look like a religious organization. Many AA members talk openly about God, prayer, miracles, God's will, or turning things over to God's care. Most AA meetings end with a group prayer. If you have no religious background or have had a negative religious experience in the past, this can be enough to send you right back out the door of the meeting place. Let's take a closer look at what underlies this religious talk that is so much a part of AA.

One of the core beliefs operating in AA is that alcoholics cannot quit drinking on their own power. Your own experience is likely a testimony to the failure of personal willpower. If you could have quit drinking on your own, you would have done so a long time ago, before it caused the damage to yourself, your relationships, or other aspects of your life that brought you to this point. It isn't that you don't have enough willpower; the problem can't be solved by willpower. One way of expressing this is to say, "I can't solve this problem myself."

However, millions of people have successfully quit drinking through AA. They suggest relying on something outside of yourself and beyond your own personal strength. Many AA members call this a Higher Power. For some, it makes sense to see this Higher Power as God and to bring their religious traditions to that relationship. For others, their Higher Power is simply the connection with other people who share the same problem, all of whom are trying to get and stay sober; in AA they refer to that as "the fellowship."

It is not the goal of AA to convert you to any particular religious belief system. It is one of the few places that people from many faiths, and some with no traditional religious ideas, can gather together and talk openly about their beliefs. The variety of Higher Powers in one AA meeting can be remarkable. You might have a person who uses the AA group as her Higher Power sitting next to a Catholic priest who uses his religious belief in God as his Higher Power sitting next to a woman who believes in a concept of Nature as her Higher Power.

In the United States, Christianity is one of the most widespread religions, and the same is true in AA in the United States. Does this mean you have to be Christian to be in AA? Absolutely not. Do you have to believe in God to attend AA? No way. Do you have to have a personal concept of a Higher Power to attend AA? No. Eventually, if you decide to follow the suggestions of the AA program, you will develop your own belief system and learn how to develop a connection with your own

Higher Power. It isn't something you are expected to have or understand before you walk in the door.

What to Expect in an AA Meeting

AA is a community with its own rituals, beliefs, and practices. Knowing what these are ahead of time can make your first meeting much more comfortable.

What Is the Difference Between an Open Meeting and a Closed Meeting?

Sometimes, people who do not have drinking problems themselves are interested in attending AA, but allowing them to come as observers threatens the anonymous aspect of the program. This is dealt with by offering some meetings that are open to the general public. Anyone can attend an "open" meeting. A student writing a paper about AA, a family member seeking information to help a loved one, or a therapist wanting to know more about how AA can help his or her clients would be welcome at these meetings. Closed meetings, on the other hand, are strictly for people who have a desire to stop drinking themselves. Since you meet the membership requirement of AA, which is "a desire to stop drinking," you are free to attend either open or closed meetings. The AA meeting list (which you'll learn about later in this chapter) will generally designate which meetings are open and which are closed.

The Two Types of Meetings

AA meetings come in two basic formats, a speaker meeting and a discussion meeting. A speaker meeting is similar to a presentation, in which one AA member, or sometimes two or three in a row, stand in the front of the room, often at a podium, and share about their experiences with drinking and sobriety. Everyone else in the room is an audience member. The speakers are almost always chosen ahead of time. (It is not likely that a stranger would approach you and ask you to be the speaker, but if this were to happen you could just turn him or her down.)

Speaker-style meetings are often the most comfortable for people who are just getting sober because you are not expected to introduce yourself or talk about yourself. You could arrive, speak to no one, sit near the back, and leave immediately after the meeting has concluded. A benefit of a speaker-style meeting is that you are able to hear an overview of someone else's experience, including what methods he or she tried that didn't work and how he or she finally achieved sobriety. Many times, you will find yourself identifying with things the speaker says, which will help you come to terms with your own problems and addiction. Try to focus on these similarities between yourself and the speaker, rather than the ways you are different from each other.

Discussion meetings involve more personal talk. Typically, a chairperson will start the meeting, which might involve making some announcements and reading a section from the book titled *Alcoholics Anonymous*, which is known by people in AA as "the Big Book." Usually the section of the book that is read at the start of a meeting is from the opening pages of Chapter 5, "How It Works." People may be sitting around a table or spread throughout a room in a roughly circular seating arrangement. Sometimes, because of the way the room is set up, all the people may be facing the front of the room.

After the chairperson has made the announcements and read "How It Works," he or she will usually announce a topic that the meeting will focus on that week. These topics are usually tied directly to some concept in AA and are generally open ended. For instance, the topic one week may be cravings. Another time it might be gratitude. Often the topic is one of the Twelve Steps of AA, so the chairperson might say the topic this week is Step Three. You will notice, as the meeting progresses, that some people try to focus on the topic and others do not. It is not required that people stick to the topic.

Once the topic has been established, the chairperson either will talk about how he or she relates to that particular topic or will ask someone else to be the first to share this week. This begins the discussion portion of the meeting. Several methods may be employed for moving the discussion around to different members. Most commonly, people go in the order in which they are seated. After one person is done talking, it is expected the person next to that person will introduce himself or herself and take a turn. This opportunity to talk continues to move around the room until either everyone has had a chance to talk or until the meeting is over.

What If I Don't Want to Talk?

Some meetings are run in such way that everyone who is there will get a chance to talk no matter how long it takes. Other meetings have established a start and end time and will end promptly even if not everyone has spoken. Some meetings have a tradition in which the person who is finishing speaking will call on someone to speak next. In this type of meeting, you don't know who will talk next. Because they are calling on people by name, you are not likely to be called on because they don't know your name yet. Occasionally you'll run into an unconventional approach to calling on people. For example, one meeting may hand out ticket stubs and draw the ticket numbers out of a can. If your number is selected, it is your turn to speak.

Whatever the tradition is at a particular meeting for passing around the turn to speak, *you can always choose not to talk*. If it is your turn and you want to remain silent, you can handle it several ways. You can simply say, "I pass." This is acceptable, although it can make you seem unfriendly or guarded. Instead, you might consider saying your first name and explaining that you are new and are just here to listen this time. Almost always, the group will accept this graciously and move along. They might welcome you or encourage you to come back. If you pass or say you are new, it increases the likelihood that members will approach you after the meeting to introduce themselves and offer support.

What Else Can I Expect at a Meeting?

At some point during the meeting, a basket or coffee can may be passed around for donations. These donations pay for the rental of the room and the supply of coffee and any AA literature that is available. Feel free to donate a dollar or two if you choose. There is no obligation to do so.

Meetings usually close with a prayer. Typically, those in attendance stand up, hold hands in a circle, and recite a prayer out loud together. This might be the Lord's Prayer, or it might be the Serenity Prayer. You are not required to participate in this ritual, but you will draw more attention to yourself by not doing so than by doing so. Many choose to join the circle but remain silent through the prayer. Often a group has some saying they like to repeat at the end of the prayer, a little chant of encouragement such as "Keep coming back, it works."

Some meetings offer a free copy of *Alcoholics Anonymous*, or the Big Book. If it is not offered for free, see if they have any copies available for purchase. If you have any difficulty finding one at a meeting, try a local bookstore or order one through one of the Internet bookstores. If finances are a concern, this would be a good opportunity for you to make use of the library card that you gathered with the rest of your materials.

When you start attending AA, gather any free materials that are available. These items, along with your copy of the Big Book, will be part of your sobriety supplies.

You may have the idea that AA meetings always take place in smoke-filled rooms and that the participants chain-smoke throughout the meeting. In fact, many if not most AA meetings are now nonsmoking meetings, and they often take place where smoking indoors is not allowed, such as in a conference room in a church or business. A room where smoking is allowed can, in fact, get pretty cloudy during a meeting. When you get an AA schedule, see if the meetings are designated as "smoking" and "nonsmoking" meetings. Even if you are a smoker, you might prefer the nonsmoking meetings.

I'm Still Not Sure It's for Me . . .

Even if you feel reluctant to attend AA and you question how it could benefit you, please try it. Look up "Alcoholics Anonymous" in the phone book. Call and ask for some times and locations of meetings today and over the next couple of days. Ask them to mail you a list of all of the meetings in your area or to tell you how to find the local AA schedule online. Then, rather than waiting for the list to arrive in the mail, go to one of the meetings you heard about in that phone call. While at the meeting, ask for a current meeting list. This list is one of the most important pieces of literature you will ever pick up at an AA meeting. It will give you the days of the week, times, and locations of all of the AA meetings in your area. This way, you can not only try out a variety of meetings to find a "home group" that you feel comfortable with but will also know exactly where to go if you really need to get to a meeting as soon as possible.

You may not like the first meeting you attend. Luckily, each meeting site seems to have its own personality. One AA meeting, for instance the Thursday night group, may have a reputation for being very spiritual. Another, maybe the Saturday morning meeting, might pride itself on the good sense of humor displayed by the people who regularly attend. In larger metropolitan areas, you'll often find AA groups aimed at men only or women only, AA groups held in Spanish or Chinese, or AA groups that address the unique needs of gays and lesbians or of younger people.

You will need to shop around and try several meetings before you figure out which ones you like the best and where you feel most comfortable. When you first quit drinking, if you are not in residential treatment or in a detoxification facility, it is recommended that you attend an AA meeting every single day. This may seem extreme to you. However, most AA meetings only last one hour. If you go every day, that will be seven hours a week in AA meetings. Chances are that in the past you spent more than seven hours a week drinking. It is not unreasonable to spend at least that much time learning about sobriety and meeting people who have successfully quit drinking.

I Have a Drinking Problem, but I Don't Think I Am an Alcoholic

One common misconception about AA is that you have to call yourself an alcoholic in order to participate. It is true that the vast majority of those in attendance do refer to themselves as alcoholics, or sometimes as an alcoholic/addict if the person has a drug addiction in addition to alcohol. However, the only requirement for membership in AA is a desire to quit drinking. You do not have to introduce yourself as alcoholic, you do not need to stay sober, and you don't have to buy into the AA ideas. All they ask of you as you walk through the door is that you want to quit drinking. If you didn't have that, you wouldn't have read this far.

It can be awkward, however, if everyone else is going around the room saying "I'm Mary Beth and I'm an alcoholic" or "I'm Roberto and I'm an alcoholic" and you don't intend to say the same about yourself. One way to feel more comfortable is to plan out ahead of time what you will say when it comes to you. "Hi, I'm Todd and I don't know if I'm an alcoholic or not" would work just fine. So would, "I'm Li and this is my first meeting." Or you could try "I'm Amy and I am new in AA" or even "I'm Joe, and I'm grateful to be here."

What Benefits Can I Expect from AA?

You can increase the benefits of your involvement in AA several ways. Try to arrive at least ten minutes early and talk with others who arrive early. When the meeting ends, don't bolt out the door and disappear. Hang around for a while, talk with others, and be friendly. One phrase you might hear refers to people who are part of the "20/20 club"—these are the smart ones who arrive twenty minutes early and stay twenty minutes after the meeting has ended to socialize and meet other people.

If anyone at AA offers you his or her phone number, accept it. Take it home and add that name and number to your support list. Call the person the next day just to say "thank you" for reaching out to you. If you get invited to go out with a group of members after an AA meeting, accept the offer. These informal social gatherings, known as "fellowship," are where you can really build your support system and meet kind, warm, funny, and interesting people who don't drink.

Occasionally in AA you might run across someone who is offering you his or her phone number for the wrong reason. The person may be interested in developing a connection with you other than a shared interest in sobriety, such as romance. You will likely be able to sense this. There is no need to call the person later to thank him or her. In fact, it is best to avoid starting any romantic interests during your first thirty days of sobriety. Your decision to quit drinking, and all that goes along with that decision, should be your main priority right now. If you are searching for a relationship, you would be advised to put that search on hold for a while. Your sobriety has to be your central focus at this point in your life in order for you to accomplish it successfully.

6

Preparing for Sobriety and Dealing with Cravings

Reviewing the material we have covered so far (or will cover shortly), you should have gathered the supplies in the following list:

- A notebook or blank journal
- A couple of good pens
- Bottled water in convenient sizes
- A phone book
- A three-by-five-inch index card
- A library card
- An AA meeting list (which may still be on its way to you in the mail)

- A book titled *Alcoholics Anonymous*, otherwise known as the Big Book, as well as other AA-related literature
- A membership card to a movie rental business (discussed in Chapter 9)

Also by now, you have accomplished the following things:

- Developed your list of "Ways I Have Tried to Cut Down or Control My Drinking"
- Developed your support list and found all the phone numbers and e-mail addresses
- Called some of the people on your support list to ask for their help
- Gave away or sent into storage any alcohol-related memorabilia or equipment
- Scoured your house, garage, shed, vehicle, and workplace to find and dispose of all the alcohol
- Read about withdrawal and made responsible medical plans for dealing with withdrawal
- Called AA to get meeting information and request a list
- Cleaned and reorganized your favorite drinking spot in the house or garage
- Considered and explored your options for professional treatment

Getting on the Wagon

If you have already quit drinking, you may skip this section. If you are still drinking, it is time to make a decision. You have considered quitting, you have been reading about how to get sober, and you have plenty of good reasons to stop. You may have attended a few AA meetings to see what they are like and whether they are for you. But for some people, taking that actual step into sobriety can be intimidating. The thing that holds some people back is the fear that they won't succeed once they try. This is a valid fear, since some people don't successfully stay sober. However, if you never try to quit, the eventual outcome is the same as if you tried and failed: you're still drinking. By making the attempt, you increase your odds of actually getting sober.

Make the Decision Now

Getting sober is not a one-shot opportunity. If you quit but then begin drinking again later, you can start over. You will have learned some things about what works and what doesn't work for you, and you will have identified weak areas where you need to shore up your support. You might even come to recognize that you need more structure than you previously realized and may make a decision to get treatment or to increase your involvement in treatment.

You might not have a fear of failing but a fear of succeeding. If you get sober and it works out for you, alcohol will no longer be a part of your life. You may be concerned about how much you are going to miss it and worry that your life will be unhappy without the drinking. You might panic at the thought of a life entirely without alcohol.

It may be difficult to face that your life, with alcohol in it, is not actually working out that well. If your drinking is enough of a problem that you are reading this book, then it is pretty likely that it is causing problems for you in at least one, and more likely several, areas. Your boss, your kids, your banker, your mom, or your own body might be anxious for you to quit. You fear being unhappy if you quit drinking, but even with alcohol, you are probably not experiencing a great deal of happiness. If you are like most people who are worried about their own drinking, the addiction has you tied up in knots. Getting sober will end up feeling like a relief to you, once you get past the most difficult first few days.

Make a decision. You could decide that you are done drinking as of right now, even if you have already been drinking today. You could decide that starting tomorrow, you are going to begin using the ideas you have been reading about and quit entirely. Pick a day, and don't put it off too long. Selecting a date three months from now is not very workable. Choose to stop today or at some point in the very near future. Gather the supplies listed above if you haven't done so already, be sure you understand the dangers of withdrawal, start developing your support list, and establish your quit date. Do it now.

Cravings: How to Resist the Urge to Drink

One of the most difficult aspects of getting sober, during withdrawal and after the acute symptoms subside, is experiencing cravings. Cravings are strong urges for alcohol. They often feel like an obsession with alcohol or an incredibly strong desire to drink. You are likely to experience cravings even if you have firmly decided that you don't want to drink again.

In the first few days of sobriety, cravings can be related to withdrawal. Your body is asking for a substance that it has grown accustomed to receiving. But even after any physical withdrawal has passed, you may continue to feel cravings. One reason for this is that you have relied on alcohol for a variety of purposes up until now, and when those situations occur where you would have used alcohol in the past, it can trigger a craving. For instance, maybe you have used alcohol to deal with stress. If this is true, then anytime you are in a stressful situation you might experience a craving. Perhaps you have used alcohol to relax. In that case, you may experience cravings at the time of day when you feel it is time to unwind. Drinkers who have relied on alcohol to make socializing more comfortable might notice their cravings just before or during a social event.

While some cravings are predictable, others seem to come out of nowhere. You may be feeling fine and not be experiencing anything particularly stressful. Still, a craving can spring up anyway. It may have been triggered by some event that happened yesterday or the day before. Maybe you heard a beer commercial on the radio earlier in the week and didn't realize it. Often cravings just happen, with no logical explanation. You should expect to have these cravings. Even if you don't have any at first, you are very likely to have some eventually, and you need to be prepared for them. If you don't respond to a craving effectively, it can lead you back into drinking. You need to have several different techniques at your disposal for getting through a period of craving without drinking.

Beating a Craving

As soon as you realize that you are having a craving, start drinking water. Don't substitute cola, tea, or coffee. Just drink some water. Two large glasses is recommended. Sometimes being dehydrated can trigger a craving, and if you can get properly hydrated quickly, the craving will often disappear.

The next step for dealing with a craving is to reveal the craving to someone who supports your plan to get sober. Often just admitting that you feel like drinking can reduce the intensity of the desire. Call someone from your support list, call the AA phone number, or call someone you met at an AA meeting. If you get no answer when you call someone, keep going down your list until you are able to reach someone. Tell him or her you are feeling like drinking and ask the person to talk to you for a while until the feeling passes.

One of the best responses to a craving is to attend an AA meeting. (This is not always possible, since some cravings occur while you are at work or late at night.) This is where your AA meeting list comes in handy. If it is possible, head straight to an AA meeting.

Some people have experienced relief from a craving by changing their surroundings. Go for a short walk, move to a different part of the house, or go visit a person on your support list. Eating something will sometimes help as well. Another approach is to change your activity. If you are watching television, go wash the dishes. If you are working on paperwork, go outside and rake leaves or garden. A brisk walk or a hot shower might be what it takes to get your mind refocused on sobriety and to relieve your craving.

Most cravings are short lived. Remember that it will go away. Make a note in your notebook or journal about what you did to deal with the craving and how well it worked. You can refer to this when you have another craving in the future.

Analyzing the Craving

After you successfully get through a craving, you can examine whether being around alcohol had anything to do with starting the craving. Did you drive by a bar where you used to drink? Did you accidentally go down the grocery store aisle that contains alcohol? Did you hear a song that reminded you of your drinking days? Were you watching someone drink alcohol at the table next to you in a restaurant recently? In early sobriety, even being near alcohol is dangerous. You won't have to avoid being around it forever. Eventually your ability to stay sober will become more developed and you will be able to attend social functions where alcohol is present. In the first thirty days, however, you should avoid being around it entirely.

7

The Banned-from-My-Hand Rule

HERE IS a deceptively simple, powerful tool to help you achieve your goal of getting and staying completely alcohol-free. While it may seem ridiculous at first, it is actually a serious technique for creating a distinct boundary between you and any alcohol you happen to be around, at any point in your life.

Banned from My Hand

If you are serious about your decision to quit drinking, then alcohol doesn't ever belong in your hand for any reason. If you can train yourself to follow this guideline, the chances of a return to drinking are greatly reduced—one saying used in AA is that if there is no first drink, then there can't be a tenth one. Training yourself to ban alcohol from your hand will take some thought and creativity on your part.

To use this tool, start by making a decision that you are never going to handle any alcohol. Then, whenever you see some alcohol in close proximity, view it with great wariness, as though you were looking at a poisonous snake or some type of hazardous material that has spilled. By viewing it in this fashion, you can teach yourself not to reach out and "accidentally" end up with a beer or a drink in your hand. Once alcohol is in your hand, the route to your mouth is a very short trip. Holding it not only raises the possibility of drinking it but also is likely to trigger cravings, which can be set off by the familiar look, feel, and smell of the alcohol product. Therefore, you should not be the one going to the refrigerator to get a beer for someone else, and you should not be pouring the wine at a reception.

There is never any reason why alcohol should be in your hand. Another way to look at it is that you are similar to people with a severe allergy to peanuts. If the allergy is serious enough they can't even eat a product that is made in the same factory where peanuts are stored. They have to avoid inhaling tiny particles of peanuts in the air and can have a serious reaction triggered by holding a handful of peanuts. Viewing alcohol as a dangerous substance that you shouldn't even smell would benefit you greatly as a sober person.

If alcohol is never in your hand, it is more difficult to fail, since to do so would require a straw and some flexibility! If a person you live with forgets about your goal and leaves alcohol someplace where you cannot avoid seeing it, **don't touch it**. Don't even go near it. At the earliest opportunity, ask someone else to put it away, out of sight. If a waiter mixes up your order with someone else's and sets a beer in front of you, point to it and say, "That isn't mine; could you please take it away?"

You may think there are logical exceptions to this, when a sober person would need to have some type of alcohol in his or her hand at some point. The truth is, you can live a long, sober life and follow this rule every day, without ever inconveniencing yourself or others to any real degree. Eventually, you will learn to use humor and grace to avoid these situations.

The Banned-from-My-Hand rule is not something you need to announce or reveal to others. For instance, let's say you are at an event where alcohol is being served, and someone says, "Would you get me a glass of wine?" You do not need to explain that you are viewing alcohol as a poisonous snake and you aren't allowed to hold it in your hand, because frankly, that would sound a little bizarre. Just say, "Oh, sorry, I was just running to the restroom," or make some other excuse.

Another option would be to say you were going to get some appetizers and your hands would be full. Or turn to a friend sitting near you and say, "Come with me. Maybe you could help me carry things back to the table." Hopefully, you won't even have to implement this rule during your first thirty days of sobriety, since that is a time when you should work diligently to avoid being in any situations where alcohol is present. If you do come across some alcohol, you'll know a good way to deal with it, by using the Banned-from-My-Hand rule.

Religious Traditions and Alcohol

Many religions employ alcohol as part of observances or sacraments, which might seem to come into conflict with the Banned-from-My-Hand rule. If you are actively practicing a religion where this is the case, here are some thoughts about how to follow your religious teachings while following the Banned-from-My-Hand rule.

Catholic, Lutheran, Orthodox Christian, and Episcopal churches usually use wine as part of their communion services. Other Christian denominations may as well. It is generally acceptable to choose not to consume the wine. Most communion ceremonies involve both bread and wine, and choosing the bread and skipping the wine does not diminish the spiritual benefit you receive from participating in the tradition. Some non-drinkers choose to kiss or touch the chalice containing the communion wine as a way to simulate partaking, which you might consider as an option. It is also fine to pass entirely, without touching the chalice. If you are given the option of participating in communion using grape juice, this is a good choice for you.

Feel free to approach your clergy on this issue. Some will have a sound understanding of the risks you would be taking by communing with wine. Some need education on the subject, and if this is the case, try explaining your problem as something like an allergic reaction, which may help him or her grasp what you are up against.

Some conservative branches of religious denominations are quite strongly opposed to "communing under one species," which you would be doing by accepting the bread but refusing the wine. One way to adhere to these strict teachings while reducing the risk to your sobriety is to drink communion wine that has been diluted with water and to only drink one drop. The amount of wine consumed is irrelevant to the spiritual benefit of communion, so this is usually acceptable.

Certain Jewish holidays or observances involve or encourage alcohol use, such as Kiddush, Passover, and

Purim. However, it's important to keep in mind that alcohol use is never required. Anyone who might suffer harm, which includes recovering alcoholics, is exempt from this obligation. Indeed, the Code of Jewish Law explicitly says that if one suspects the drinking may affect him or her negatively, then he or she should *not* drink.

If your particular religious tradition that involves alcohol consumption isn't addressed here, seek guidance directly from your spiritual leaders. This is also a good topic to discuss with other people who are abstaining from alcohol, such as people you meet at AA meetings.

8

Staying Sober Online

IN ADDITION to the supplies we gathered in the first chapter of the book, one other tool has proven to be extremely helpful to many people while getting sober: the Internet.

The Power of the Internet

Support for your sobriety can be found at your fingertips. If you have an Internet connection or can get to a public library that supplies one, you can access the wide world of sobriety support that appears online. The benefits of doing so are that it allows you to see how widespread the problem is and how many people you share it with, and it offers countless ideas about how to address it at any time, day or night. You might also find some comfort in the fact that the Internet can be anonymous.

One of the great things about Internet sites that support recovery is that they are up and running twenty-four hours a day. If you are having a difficult time at two o'clock in the morning, you aren't likely to find an AA meeting to go to (though some do exist, in larger cities!), and you may be reluctant to call those on your support list because they are probably asleep. The Internet never sleeps, so you can always turn to recovery websites for inspiration, advice, and other people's stories that you can use as a model.

Also, many of the Internet sites allow for discussion either through message boards or live chat, so you can read and/or participate in back-and-forth conversation about important topics such as cravings and get a more in-depth sense of how to handle your feelings than you might be able to get from simply reading a book written by a single author. You can also do more than observe, by entering into these conversations and asking the questions that you want answered.

Many people find the Internet to be a great way to supplement going to outpatient services or AA meetings. You might be able to find recovery websites specifically targeted to your needs. For example, there are recovery sites dedicated to addressing the needs of gays and lesbians, single mothers, teenagers, Spanish speakers—the list goes on and on. You will be able to find some sites that are a great fit for you.

One other feature about Web-based recovery sites that can be very helpful to people is the fact that they are truly anonymous. You don't have to show up in a church basement or a meeting hall worrying about someone recognizing you as you walk in or out of the building. You don't have to use your real name, and the people you are interacting with might be from the other side of the country or the other side of the world. It's a very low-key way to ease into the idea of recovery from the comfort of your own home.

How Do I Get Started?

An easy way to begin is by using an Internet search engine such as Google.com or Yahoo.com (which you can also use to set up a free e-mail account). Try entering several combinations of sobriety-related keywords. To get started, type "alcoholism recovery." Be sure to put the phrase in quotes to narrow the search. You will see a long list of available websites. Some of them will not interest you. They might be clinical research papers, an individual's rants about treatment or AA, or scam artists trying to sell you a "painless, easy" solution to your problem. Among these, however, you will also find sites of interest, where you can learn about recovery, get support, read other people's solutions, and order tapes or CDs of speakers from AA conventions. Other keywords you might try in your Internet search are "sober support," "alcohol recovery support," or "how to stay sober." Remember that you will need to sift through the results to find the sites that have valuable information and support for you.

Some Useful Sites

Websites spring up and disappear overnight, so providing a comprehensive list of them here isn't realistic, since it will quickly be outdated. However, a few that are pretty well established may serve as a springboard to other useful sites.

Sober24.com is an Internet site that has been around for a while and provides meaningful help to people in recovery. Membership is completely free, thanks to a gift from the Evelyn Foundation. This site is easy to navigate and offers a variety of tools to help you. They have discussion forums with topics like "Weekly Topic," "Beginners and Newcomers," "Life in Recovery," "Just for Fun," "Gambling and Debt Issues," "Grief Forum," "Relationship Issues," and "Steps and Traditions."

Under any of those headings, along with other topics, you can read individual members' discussions, including their support of one another, tips and ideas for getting through difficult times, and countless suggestions about what works in sobriety. You might benefit from just reading what others have written, or you can jump in with your own issue, sharing how many days you have been sober, perhaps, or asking a question about cravings. Then, check back frequently to read responses to your issue.

Sober24.com also hosts live Internet meetings, which happen in real time. They operate like a chat room, where you can "talk" back and forth with others via the computer or just read what others are writing to one another. In addition, they have an online tool that helps you track your progress in sobriety, and you can use it to set up a "call for help" that will go out to certain people you select if you are struggling. Consider trying it, and use the people on your support list for your cyber "call for help" list, as well.

Another useful site on the Internet is The AA Grapevine Online, found at aagrapevine.org. *The Grapevine* is a magazine published by AA since 1944, in which AA members from around the world discuss or debate ideas about AA, recovery, alcoholism, and related topics. Like Sober24.com, they have discussion forums where you can scroll through other people's posts or post your own thoughts or feelings on something related to sobriety. In addition, they have a digital archive of all of the articles from *The Grapevine*, sorted by topics. To access the digital archive, you have to subscribe, which is very reasonably priced at two dollars for one month or fifteen dollars for a year. They also have a special welcome message for newcomers, with some helpful links attached.

To find and attend an AA meeting online, go to http://aa-intergroup.org and scroll down to the section that says "Looking for an Online Meeting," where you can choose between an e-mail-style meeting and a live-chat meeting. The intergroup page has other helpful links as well, and it can help you get connected fast to AA support. They have links for meetings in many languages, as well as special focus meetings such as women only or for the visually impaired.

The AA History and Trivia site, at aahistory.com, has a sobriety calculator that allows you to see how long you have been sober down to the second. It also has a wealth of materials available, including tapes and CDs of AA speakers, and a detailed history of the origins of the Serenity Prayer. At facetheissue.com/alcoholmovie.html, you can view a short, animated movie about alcoholism that is narrated by Nicole Kidman.

Online Limitations

Many recovering people feel that online involvement has greatly boosted their recovery and sense of connection to others who are going through the same thing. However, there is also a great deal of discussion about how important it is that online chat rooms and AA discussion boards should not replace face-to-face AA meetings. The reasons for this are sound. Although you can get excellent support online, the people you are interacting with are not likely to be in close geographical proximity to you, so you can't meet them for a cup of coffee, go shoot some baskets, or see a movie together—activities that really help build a sober life. To socialize with sober people, you need to make sober friends in your actual community.

9

Unexpected and Unmanageable Feelings

When you stop drinking, it is very likely that you will experience an increase in how emotional you feel. For some, this emotional upheaval might manifest itself as waves of sadness. Others might feel nervous, scared, or panicky. Anger that seems to come out of the blue is also a possibility. These new emotions can be very unsettling and difficult to deal with. Let's take a look at why these feelings are suddenly appearing and how you can manage them appropriately.

Why Am I So Moody?

The dedicated drinking you were doing in the past had a side effect of suppressing your feelings. You might not have been drinking for this purpose, but even so, regular alcohol abuse has a numbing effect on people's normal emotions. Many people end up abusing alcohol just because of this fact. Whether they are aware of it or not, they don't like how they are feeling and they drink in order to feel differently or to not feel at all.

For however long your drinking has been a problem, your emotions have been pressed down, hidden, numbed, or ignored. They haven't really had a chance at free expression, so they've been stacking up inside of you. Because the whole point of having emotions is to express them, they are waiting for their opportunity to stand up and shout. When you stop drinking, and the numbing effect of the alcohol is removed, they think this is their big chance.

Unfortunately, you might not have good coping skills for experiencing and appropriately releasing these unleashed feelings. The feelings themselves may seem new, unfamiliar, and overpowering. You might wonder what is happening to you. Here you are trying to make a healthy choice for yourself by quitting alcohol, and these unruly feelings start messing things up right away. The emotions are likely to be unwelcome, uncomfortable ones of regret, sadness, grief, irritability, and anger, even toward those on your support list or who are otherwise trying to help you. You probably wish these feelings and emotions would just go away and leave you alone. You might even be considering drinking to make them go away.

If you decide to drink to get away from the feelings, you will end up in a situation where the feelings you are trying to avoid continue to store themselves up, waiting for their chance to come out and express themselves. The more feelings you stock up, the more alcohol it takes to keep them numb. So you drink more, the feelings build up more, and the cycle continues, bringing both your drinking and your unexpressed emotions to dangerous levels. This is why drinking is not a good long-term answer to this problem.

How Long Will It Last?

The irritability and lack of patience that accompany early sobriety and reduce your ability to have fun will get better over time. You might notice a positive change on a week-by-week basis; or you might find yourself fluctuating between feelings of calm and contentment and feelings of extreme irritability. How soon it goes away forever is a very individual thing, with some people experiencing bouts of irritability for up to eighteen months. This doesn't mean they are constantly out of sorts for the first year and a half, but that it takes them that long to achieve a real sense of equilibrium.

As your own moodiness improves, your ability to enjoy both large and small recreational activities dramatically increases. What this means in early sobriety is that to some extent you should accept that things won't seem like much fun at first. Don't mistake this for a permanent situation. Many people have done so and made a decision to return to drinking because their life without alcohol seemed so miserable. Remember, your ability to find enjoyment in life will grow and grow, you won't always feel like this, and you will always feel worse if you start drinking again.

How to Deal with Unfamiliar Emotions

What can you do instead? You can approach this issue in several ways, and you may have to try a few different techniques before you find what works for you. Remember, you've been carrying these feelings around for some time, so it is also going to take some time to address them.

First of all, it is important to know that your feelings can't hurt you. They can be extremely uncomfortable, and you might really dislike them, but the feelings themselves are not dangerous. They are completely natural. You may have convinced yourself that you cannot handle any feelings. The truth is that you can survive having feelings, even if they cause you what seems like extreme discomfort.

Discomfort is something most people expect to deal with every day. Because of your overuse of alcohol, you may have forgotten how to handle day-to-day discomfort without drinking. Any amount of emotional discomfort might seem exaggerated to you. Remind yourself that you *can* tolerate discomfort, that it won't last forever, and that you can get through it without drinking.

It is helpful to think of feelings as a natural expression of our selves. Our spirits are looking for ways to express themselves, and feelings are one of the ways we do so. Expressing them is a way of releasing them and being done with them. If you have had habits of storing feelings up, ignoring them, or numbing them with alcohol, you might not have any good ways to express these newly freed feelings. Let's look at how that might be done.

Letting It Out

Feelings well up within us, but they really want to find their way out of us. When we are very sad or stressed, for example, crying is one of the ways the feeling gets expressed. The tears are a way for the feelings to travel from within to without. When you quit drinking, you may feel close to tears much more often than you used to. This does not mean you are going crazy or losing it. It means your feelings are getting closer to the surface, aren't being numbed out anymore, and want to find their way out. Allow yourself some private time and space to let those tears flow. You won't always feel this sensitive, but it is common in early sobriety.

If you have not allowed yourself to cry for some time, you may be afraid that if you start to cry you will never be able to stop. Many people have this fear in early sobriety, partly because the feelings have been stored up for so long that they feel overwhelming. The truth is that you may cry for quite a while at first, but you will not cry for the rest of your life. You may cry yourself to sleep a time or two, but the tears won't go on forever.

Write It Down or Talk It Out

Another way to express feelings is to write them down. Use your notebook from your supplies list to start writing or drawing about these new feelings you are experiencing. Consider making a daily entry in the notebook about what feelings you are noticing, what they feel like, whether they are pleasant or unpleasant, and what you are doing to deal with them. Also note any cravings. This way you can go back through the entries later and see if there is a pattern of experiencing cravings with a particular emotion or situation. Writing your feelings down may also help you gain a sense of control over your emotions, which can be a reassuring feeling.

However, the quickest, most direct, and probably most effective way to express feelings is to tell them to someone else. Call or meet with someone on your support list and tell him or her you are having a lot of new emotions and that you need to talk about them. Then tell the person about whatever you are feeling, such as loneliness, anger, fear, sadness, or happiness. Don't worry if your feelings seem irrational or fear that the person you are sharing them with will somehow judge you. Just get them out in the open.

AA meetings are the perfect place to talk about your newfound feelings. The members there have been through this wave of emotion when they quit drinking, so they can relate to you and give you tips for coping or just a sympathetic ear if that is all you need. If you are in professional treatment, be sure to tell your counselor or therapist about the feelings you are having. They are experts at teaching you how to express and manage them.

The intense feelings that you may be experiencing in the first thirty days of getting sober won't always be like this. They seem so intense because you haven't felt them in their true form in some time and because you may not have good skills for expressing them. You will begin to get used to having them, you will build those new skills, and soon your feelings will just be a normal part of your day.

The Grief That Is Tired of Waiting

A particular feeling that may surface when you quit drinking is grief. Drinking enabled you to ignore or pay less attention to the normal losses you have experienced during the months or years that you were abusing alcohol, but they didn't disappear. You may have gone through the death of someone close to you, a traumatic episode of some sort, or the breakdown of an intimate relationship or a marriage during the time that you were drinking too much. If so, it is very likely that either you never dealt with the impact of that loss or you dealt with it incompletely. Even if you can't think of a large loss you went through, grief might be something you have to wrestle with in early sobriety. Smaller issues that occurred while you were still drinking may have built up. A series of losses can have the impact of one large one. For instance, if you have lost contact with someone you cared about, lost a job you liked, and lost a pet, the combination of these losses can be the same as a significant loss such as a death of a close loved one.

Like the feelings described in the previous section, grief wants its chance to be felt and heard. It has patience and will wait around for years for the right moment to express itself. The losses you experienced while you were drinking probably did not get their proper expression. You may have used alcohol to numb the impact of the loss and to avoid the normal feelings you otherwise would have had. Unfortunately, this was only a short-term answer.

When the numbing effects of alcohol go away in the first few days of your sobriety, grief is likely to rise up and demand your attention. You may have memories and feelings come flooding back in such a way that it feels like the loss was yesterday, instead of weeks, months, or years ago. This can make you tearful, sad, tired, overwhelmed, and scared.

If grief is a significant issue in your life, you may want to seek out some services to help you deal with it. Churches and funeral homes frequently offer grief support groups, and many of them are free of charge. Many counselors specialize in assisting people with grief. It is appropriate to seek out these services even if the loss itself occurred many years ago, because the feelings of grief might still be fresh.

Is Now the Best Time?

You might think this isn't a good time to tackle the grief issues you have, since you are trying to quit drinking now and that is hard enough. However, if you have a big, unresolved grief issue, it can make sobriety very difficult. The longer you go without alcohol, the more you will feel and remember the loss. Eventually this pain and sadness can make you decide to drink again. It would be nice if you could set the grief aside while you get on your feet with sobriety, but grief is one emotion that often won't wait. When these painful feelings arise in early sobriety, it can seem like sobriety is an awful thing. You might find yourself thinking you were better off when you were drinking, because at least then you didn't have to feel all this pain. It is important to remember that these feelings are oversized and magnified because they have been ignored, avoided, or numbed until now. The pain will get smaller, and a sober life won't always feel so uncomfortable.

Avoiding Boredom

When you were drinking, much of your time was spent planning to drink, drinking, and recovering from the effects of your drinking. Now that you are getting sober, the empty time that has become available may cause problems for you, and you may find yourself feeling bored or restless. It is important that you make good choices about how to fill that time. You've already read about the importance of attending AA meetings. If you live in an area where many meetings are available, it would be best if you attended one every day. The meeting will take up one hour, plus the time getting to and from the meeting. That still leaves a lot of hours unaccounted for, however.

Spending time with people on your support list is not only good for your sobriety but also helps you begin to repair any damage that your drinking may have caused in those relationships. The people on your list obviously care about you and are happy to see you sober. They will look forward to being around you, as long as you are not drinking. It doesn't matter what kinds of activities you do together, as long as the activities don't bring you into close range of an alcohol supply. You could play cards together, work in the yard, go to the gym, take a walk, or watch a movie. What matters is that you are spending time with someone who cares about you and supports your decision to quit drinking.

Watching movies, in particular, can be a great tool for filling free time. This is where your movie rental card from your supplies list gets put to use. There are several movies about getting sober that may interest you at this point in your life. One of your first movie rentals as you get sober should be a film called *My Name is Bill W.* It is the story of how AA got started, starring James Woods as Bill Wilson (one of the founders of AA), JoBeth Williams as his wife, Lois, and James Garner as Dr. Bob (AA's other founder). This movie is likely to inspire you and will help you understand how AA was first formed.

Other movies that may interest you are *When a Man Loves a Woman*, *Clean and Sober*, and *28 Days.* Although they don't all have happy endings and might speak to drug addiction as well as alcoholism, they use both humor and drama to relay information about getting sober. But feel free to enjoy any kind of movie that will make you laugh, make you cry, or scare the pants off you, as long as it doesn't have extended scenes involving characters enjoying alcohol use.

Reading can be another positive way to use your new free time. You can educate yourself about sobriety and get ideas, direction, and strength from other people's experiences, recorded in books. Buy or check out from the library *The Recovery Book*, by Al J. Mooney, M.D., Arlene Eisenberg, and Howard Eisenberg, which is an excellent source of information that will serve you long beyond the first thirty days of your new lifestyle. AA has several books that are considered the official, approved literature of the program. You should already have a copy of *Alcoholics Anonymous*, affectionately called the

Big Book. Another book that is particularly helpful is titled *Living Sober.* It is full of practical ideas for using the AA program effectively and tells you how to deal with stumbling blocks in your sobriety.

One type of book that is very popular among people who have quit drinking is a daily reflection or daily meditation book. These books have a short, reflective reading for each day of the year. They might also have a relevant quote on each page or an affirmation or short prayer. There is quite a selection, so look around at the library or bookstore. Some to look for are *Each Day a New Beginning: Daily Meditations for Women* by Karen Casey and *Touchstones: A Book of Daily Meditations for Men* by David Spohn. *Twenty-Four Hours a Day* is the AA-approved daily meditation book and is for both men and women.

Easy Does It

One danger to be aware of as you are deciding how to use your new free time is "making up for lost time." You might have many projects that have either never been started or were started but never finished. You might think this is a good time to catch up on all of those tasks that have been nagging at you.

Although it is good to start putting your life and your house in order, be careful not to exhaust yourself.

You can't catch up on everything you may have neglected in just a few short weeks. As your sobriety stretches into months and years, there will be plenty of time to take care of those unfinished obligations. It is OK to start attending to some of those things now, but don't work around the clock trying to right everything in your life. You need time to relax, play, think, and talk with others. Don't work yourself down to the bone.

10

Drinking Triggers

CERTAIN SITUATIONS or events may stir up cravings to drink, especially when you are new to sobriety. People in recovery often refer to these as "triggers," because they can quite literally trigger a drinking episode. Many have found it helpful to learn about possible triggers before they occur, and avoid them if possible, to protect their sobriety.

Types of Triggers

Some triggers are common among people with drinking problems—stress, holidays, loneliness, or seeing other people drinking. Other triggers are more personal—hearing a song that you associate in your mind with drinking, having the house to yourself, or cooking spaghetti, for example. In order to learn about your own triggers, it will be helpful to think of them in two categories.

Tornado Triggers

Tornado-style triggers are big events that almost anyone can see would be a problem. Examples of tornado triggers are losing your job, experiencing the death of someone close to you, losing your possessions in a house fire, or the sudden end to an intimate relationship. These loom large on the horizon, can be unpredictable, and threaten to wreck anything in their path.

When the Warning Sirens Sound. Tornado triggers are usually out of our control and can't be avoided. If a tornado trigger occurs while you are in your first thirty days of sobriety, you will need to get extra help in order to make it through the event without drinking. That extra help might be going to more AA meetings, accessing professional counseling, or increasing your current involvement in your treatment program. For instance, if you have been going to outpatient treatment once a week and an event like this happens, you might move into an intensive outpatient program for a few weeks, which meets three times per week. The extra support can help you get through the traumatic event without giving in to a desire to drink.

Another way to get extra help after a tornado trigger event occurs is to reach out to the people on your support list. Make sure they know what happened, and talk to them about how it makes you feel. Let them know if there is anything they can do to help you—from staying with them for a few days to asking them to call you a few times a day to cooking a few meals for you.

This would also be a time when having a sponsor in AA would come in very handy. Typically a person with more than a year of sobriety, a sponsor is just another AA member, like yourself, who has more experience with sobriety than you do. Your sponsor can provide support and encouragement through a tornado trigger, and it might be just what you need to see you through. Read more about sponsors, and how to get one for yourself, in Chapter 13.

Be sure to discuss with those people on your support list—especially your sponsor if you have one—any thoughts you are having about drinking as a result of the trigger event.

Termite Triggers

Now let's discuss the other type of trigger. These are small, seemingly innocent events or actions that don't appear to cause your sobriety any serious difficulty. In fact, you may see them as little challenges to strengthen or test your resolve, and you feel proud of yourself when you've overcome them. An example would be to go into one of the environments where you used to drink and spend time with others who are drinking, while you have a glass of iced tea. Many people in early sobriety don't recognize that this type of activity can be a trigger for drinking. They tell themselves how great it was that they were able to do it successfully, and they have a tendency to congratulate themselves on how well they did. They might say, "I didn't even feel like drinking! I can do that any time! I'm cured!"

This is a termite-style trigger. Termites often do their damage long before they are ever detected. A house that has been ravaged by termites might look solid and safe, but in reality it is slowly being eaten away. It is vulnerable, even though it doesn't look it.

One termite alone can't do much damage, and it certainly takes termites quite some time to take down a house. They are, after all, pretty small creatures. However, in numbers, and over time, the damage they create can be extensive and costly. The same is true with these small triggers. Examples include watching a beer commercial; being invited to a drinking event where many people you know will be drinking, even if you don't attend; telling stories about funny things that happened when you were drinking in the past; having a dream about drinking; and hearing music that reminds you of times you drank.

While these events might seem pretty minor, they build up slowly over time and can weaken your resolve. Let's take the first example, of drinking iced tea in a place where you used to drink alcohol. You might do this successfully the first time or even several times. It gives you a sense of confidence—perhaps you would think, "I can still hang out with my drinking buddies and have a good time. Nothing has changed. Things are going to be OK." You might begin to tell yourself that being around alcohol doesn't bother you at all.

In part, you may tell yourself these things because you really don't want to have to give up those friends or that familiar social environment. If you could safely drink iced tea there, you could easily trick yourself into thinking it is a safe place for you to be; that you can handle it; that you can come by every night just for a glass or two of iced tea. You might start to overlook the risks or decide they don't apply to you. In that case, two things are likely to happen, both of which are dangerous to your sobriety.

Termites Go Unnoticed When Your Guard Is Down. The first thing that is likely to happen when you think the risks don't apply to you is that you will continue to go to that place, whether it is a bar, a friend's house, or the neighbor's body shop. If you are there regularly, then you are likely to be there at some point when your guard is down. Maybe you've had a good day and really feel like celebrating, or you've had a particularly bad day when some difficult news was delivered to you. You go to this drinking place to get support from your friends there, but the next thing you know, you end up drinking. A friend may suggest that one drink wouldn't kill you, or may tell you that you simply can't toast to a success with a glass of ginger ale. If the alcohol is within reach, it is much easier to make an impulsive decision to drink.

Termites Attack Slowly and Steadily over Time. Secondly, many people find that the time they spend around alcohol in their previous drinking environments doesn't seem to affect them at the time, but it can trigger strong cravings within a day or two. You might not feel any desire to drink when you are with your colleagues at happy hour on Monday, but you get a sudden urge to have a beer on Thursday afternoon. You might have trouble putting the two events together at first and will say the strong cravings came "out of the blue." After some exploration, however, you might discover that although there may not have been an identifiable trigger on that day, you can look back a day or two and pinpoint a time when you were around alcohol or talking with old friends about fun you had while drinking.

In this way, the trigger can act like a termite infestation. It enters when you are not suspecting it and does its damage in slow or subtle ways so that when the house falls down around you, you wonder what went wrong. Because these trigger events seem harmless when they are happening, it is very hard to identify them yourself. This is an area of recovery in which you really must rely on the experience of others who have struggled before you and learn from what they learned.

Some people are told their house has termites, but because they can't see the termites themselves, they don't believe it. The house looks fine. The doors still open, and the windows still close. However, you have to keep in mind that the loss of structural strength can't always be seen from the outside. Although it is difficult to trust other people when you are making decisions about your own life, if you are taking advice from people who have long-term sobriety and who seem to have relatively happy lives, then maybe they know something that you do not; maybe they can spot the trouble with your foundation, at least at this stage of your sobriety. One day, you will have your own success story to share with people who are new in sobriety, and you will be glad if they can learn from your experience. But for now, rely on the wisdom of people who are achieving what you hope to do, as well.

Common Termite-Style Triggers. So, what are some of these termite-style triggers? The most common ones include the following:

- Billboard, television, and radio ads for alcohol
- Listening to music that makes you sad or reminds you of your drinking days
- Not getting enough sleep
- Letting yourself get overly hungry
- Watching other people drink
- Looking at old photographs or home movies of times when you were drinking
- Driving by your favorite bar or liquor store
- Mowing the grass on a hot day
- Coming in from the cold
- Holidays, especially Independence Day, New Year's Eve, and St. Patrick's Day
- Birthdays
- High school reunions
- Old friends coming into town
- Good news (such as getting a raise)
- Wedding receptions
- Weather issues, such as a rainy weekend

Avoiding Termite Triggers. Termite triggers can largely be avoided or planned for in advance. Simply turning the channel when an alcohol commercial comes on will take care of that trigger. In your first thirty days of sobriety, decide not to attend any wedding receptions or other large celebrations. If a close relative is getting married, attend the ceremony but skip the reception. If your high school reunion is happening just as you are getting sober, miss it this time. When a song comes on the radio that reminds you of a long-lost love or reminds you of your drinking days, turn to another station. If it is your job to mow the lawn and it is a hot day, stock up on cold drinks like bottled water, juice, or soda so you will have "a cold one" that isn't a beer to consume when you are done with the lawn work.

You should also plan for how you will celebrate good news that comes your way. Ideas for alcohol-free ways to celebrate include getting a massage, ordering in some great food from a local restaurant, watching a sunset with a friend, buying a piece of jewelry, or having a special dessert. If none of these activities appeal to you, think of some others, or ask people who are nondrinkers what they do to mark special events. It may be that you've never celebrated something before without the use of alcohol, so this will be a learning experience for you. Make a list of any ideas that you like, and keep the list handy. You may need the reminders later on, when you feel like celebrating.

It's Not Just About Drinking

Keep in mind that intense experiences that put you at risk for drinking can also trigger you to abandon your newly established good habits, falling into your old, more comfortable behaviors. Increases in other addictive behaviors, such as smoking, overeating, or spending money recklessly are likely at this point. This is a prime risk time, as well, for forgetting to eat well, drink enough water, and get the appropriate amount of rest. Your response to the trigger event might not actually be drinking, but without watching carefully, your natural response might be behaviors that eventually lead back to drinking. It can be a very vulnerable spot, especially in the first thirty days. Be careful to take good care of yourself during this especially difficult time.

Why Me? Why Now?

In an ideal world, you could set aside the first thirty days of sobriety as a time when bad things couldn't happen, insulating you from negative experiences as you focus on learning how to stay sober. In fact, it may seem like the opposite—that it's only when you decide to stop drinking and feel as though you are at your weakest that bad things start to happen. Quitting alcohol doesn't cause these events, and drinking won't prevent them, but it can sure seem that way at first. Many people complain that just when they were trying to put their life together and get sober, other bad things overwhelmed them. Let's look at why that might happen.

Most people don't decide to get sober when life is going well. The negative consequences of their alcohol use have been increasing and piling up, so that many areas of life are in serious jeopardy by the time they decide to give up drinking. This might include relationships, finances, and job status. Every aspect of your life has probably been feeling the strain of your drinking problem. Just because you make a decision to quit drinking doesn't mean that those issues are going to disappear overnight. Maybe things were pushed too far before you quit drinking and the results are apparent only after you quit and are able to judge things clearly for the first time.

Negative events can be particularly discouraging to the person in early sobriety. Just when you've made a positive decision for your future and have been working hard to learn how to stay sober, complications arise or become apparent to you for the first time. If you are unprepared for this, it can be a definite trigger for returning to drinking. It would be best to plan ahead and prepare yourself for a potential stressful event, even though you might not be able to predict exactly what it will be or when it will happen. Chances are, some aspect of your drinking will catch up to you during your first thirty days—you might realize that you have no more money left in your checking account; you might notice for the first time that you have shooting pains in your back; your boyfriend or girlfriend might stop returning your calls. If you have some kind of plan in place, you are much more likely to get through the crisis without drinking.

The Trigger Lock

If you think of the stressful event as a trigger, you can think of the plan as a trigger lock. In the world of firearms, a trigger lock is a device installed around the trigger of the gun that prevents it from being fired accidentally. It is a safety device that anticipates the possibility of the unexpected happening, such as having the gun fall into the hands of young children. You can plan for the unexpected in your sobriety by designing your personal trigger locks.

Get your three-by-five-inch index card from your supplies and fold it in half down the center. Position it like a book, with the fold on the left, and write "Trigger

Locks" on the front. Open it up and write down a list of five to ten steps you can take right away if your sobriety is at great risk. If you write down people's names that could help you, be sure to include their phone numbers. If you write down something generic like "go to an AA meeting," add the phone number for an AA hotline so you can access meeting information in a pinch. If going for a walk is one of your trigger locks, consider writing down exactly where you would walk and for how long. Make sure the walking route doesn't take you past a liquor store or bar or by the home of a drinking buddy. The more clear and specific you can be with your trigger locks list, the more helpful it will be to you when you really need it. If you have "pray" as one of your trigger locks, mention a specific prayer (the Serenity Prayer, for instance), or type of prayer (something like "pray for help staying sober for the next hour"), or somewhere you can go to pray (for example, "the church on 48th and Elm is open until 10:00"). If you list "meditate," add the name of a meditation tape or CD you could use, and note exactly where you'll sit as you do it. The trigger locks are a way for you to protect yourself against drinking, and the better you design them, the better they'll work for you.

It is important that your trigger locks are actions rather than thoughts. It will make you feel better to have something to actually do, rather than just "think about your family" or "remember the last time you got drunk." Although these can be helpful, it is better to have actions such as "drink two glasses of water" or "walk for twenty minutes." Once you have filled the inside of the index card with trigger locks, fold it again along the crease and turn the card over, so you are looking at the back of it. Here, write down "It is important to me to stay sober because ______________________________." Fill in the blank with two of your top reasons for getting sober. Think about your family, your friends, your health, the job you love, the people or pets who are important to you. These are the things to focus on here.

Carry your trigger locks list with you at all times, and glance over it every couple of days. This way, you remind yourself that it exists, you will mentally prepare yourself that triggers may very well happen, and you will be more likely to remember to use it when you need to. When you get in a rough spot and the urge to drink is strong, pull it out and do several of the things you have listed. Keep doing them for as long as necessary to get through the rough time.

Your Personal Triggers

What are *your* personal triggers? You can use this next section to identify some of them, but others will come up over time, and as you learn about them, add them to your list. No matter how thorough your list is, at some point in your sobriety something will happen, large or small, that triggers a craving in you and wasn't on your list. When that occurs, just add the trigger to your list and use your trigger locks to address it.

Get out a piece of paper and write "I especially liked to drink . . ." across the top of it. Now, make a list of all the times and situations you can think of when you especially liked to drink. Your list will be unique to you, but an example could look like this:

I Especially Liked to Drink

- When I got off work
- On Friday nights
- On payday
- When I was on a road trip
- When I was doing housework
- With the guys
- After I argued with someone
- On dates
- At a bar
- With pizza
- By myself

Next, rewrite the list with a new title at the top: "My Personal Triggers." Take the information directly from your first list, with minor adjustments to the wording. "When I got off work" would become "Getting off work." "On dates" would become "dating." This is your list of personal triggers. For instance, based on the list above, you would come up with:

My Personal Triggers

- Getting off work
- Friday evenings
- Having money in my pocket
- Driving
- Cleaning house
- Hanging out with friends
- Fighting
- Dating
- Spending time at a bar
- Eating pizza
- Spending too much time alone

Consider asking people from your support list to help you add anything to your personal triggers list that you may have overlooked.

Living with Your Triggers

A person with the preceding sample list has identified eleven personal triggers that he or she will need to avoid or plan for in early sobriety. In this case, he or she can decide not to order pizza for at least the first month; make a special plan for payday such as meeting with someone from his or her support list or going to an AA function; stay away from dating for a while; don't go on any road trips, or only go with people on the support list or people who are also sober. He or she can ask a friend to help with housework or can make a plan to clean house and then meet a sober person for lunch right afterward.

Pay attention to any triggers that are likely to happen together. More than one trigger at the same time can make staying sober particularly difficult. For instance, if the person with the sample list gets paid on a Friday at the end of the workday and then goes out for pizza, he or she will have four triggers happening all at once (getting off work, getting paid, Friday night, and eating pizza). You might not think of going out for a pizza as a big deal, but in this case, it would be asking for trouble. Your personal triggers list may have many more than eleven items on it, and you will need to use your creativity to come up with ways to plan for or avoid these triggers. Remember, even if you think you can handle some of them, like getting a pizza, it could still have a "termite effect" on your sobriety.

11

Staying in Balance Physically

THE PROCESS of getting and staying sober is in many ways a process of staying in balance. How you eat and sleep are important factors that can support or sabotage your sobriety, and they must be addressed head-on in these early days of sobriety.

A Good Night's Sleep

It is possible that you have used alcohol as a sleep aid, which means you may have trouble getting to sleep during the first few weeks after your last drink. Although this is normal, it can be troubling and can contribute to feeling irritable or overwhelmed. You can do several things to get your sleep patterns adjusted naturally.

The Concern About Caffeine

In the past you may have been able to tolerate large doses of caffeine, but that is because you were counteracting its effect with alcohol. Now that the alcohol is not in your system, the caffeine is more likely to cause sleep problems for you. Limit your caffeine consumption to the first half of the day. Since coffee is the beverage of choice served at most AA meetings, be sure to take along a bottle of water when you go to evening meetings.

Get Moving

Try to get some amount of physical exercise during the day, even if it is something as simple as walking around the block. This will help your body feel as though it has exerted itself and deserves to sleep. Don't do this exercise too close to bedtime, though, as it can get your adrenaline going, which would make sleep more difficult.

The Power of Water and Sound

A hot bath or shower before bed helps relax your muscles and triggers the brain to think about relaxing as well. Playing soothing music, sitting in a dark room, or listening to a meditation tape or compact disc can also induce a restful state. If you find you are experiencing a lot of difficulty getting to sleep, consider buying a tape or CD that is specifically aimed at helping people get to sleep. These use the power of suggestion to tell your brain to relax and allow you to drift off to sleep. Some people find machines that generate "white noise" or the sound of water falling or birds chirping conducive to a good night's rest.

Avoid Chemical Sleeping Aids

Be very wary of using any kind of chemical to assist you in sleeping. Even over-the-counter products can be dangerous to your sobriety at this early stage. Remember that you are trying to learn how to function without the aid of mood-altering substances, so getting to sleep through natural means should be one of your goals.

If you try all of these suggestions and are still having sleep issues, be aware that the problems will get better as you get further into your sobriety. Some sleep problems may just be something that you have to deal with in the first few days or weeks. If you simply cannot deal with it, you could ask your doctor to prescribe something nonaddictive for a very short period, such as two or three weeks. If you take this route, be sure to tell your doctor about your drinking history and that you are now getting sober.

Disturbed Sleep

Once you've solved the problem of getting to sleep, you may notice that your sleep is disturbed by restlessness and vivid dreams. Some notice a marked increase in strange dreams in early sobriety. People commonly dream that they drank and wake up feeling upset that they blew their sobriety. These happen with such regularity that they are frequently discussed in AA meetings, where they are referred to as drinking dreams. They will occur less frequently as you build up more sober time but can happen occasionally to people with many years of sobriety. One way to look at it is that if you didn't care about your sobriety, the dreams wouldn't upset you; so being unsettled by them is a sign that you are invested in your new way of life.

What to Eat

Your food choices can also be an aid or a hindrance to your decision to quit drinking. Overeating, undereating, or making consistently poor nutritional choices will make you feel off-balance or out of whack physically, and this can lead to cravings. Also, if you allow your blood sugar levels to get too low, you can experience confusion that can lead to bad decisions.

Eating five or six small meals throughout the day may help your blood sugar levels stay more even and can decrease cravings. For the same reason, try to avoid foods with high sugar content. Be sure to consume some protein such as meat, nuts, or dairy at regular intervals throughout the day. If you have had poor eating habits in association with your drinking, make a special effort to include fruits, vegetables, and protein in your daily diet now.

Many dedicated drinkers have nutritional deficits when they finally quit drinking. You might have avoided food in order to drink more or to increase the effects of the alcohol you were consuming. Nausea may have contributed to your skipping meals. The alcohol itself has so many calories that you may not have felt hungry. This means you may be low in some essential vitamins and minerals.

Those deficiencies can cause you to feel weak, out of sorts, irritable, or tired. It is possible that they can also cause cravings. As part of your long-term sobriety, you will likely get your eating adjusted in a healthy way. At this crucial beginning point, however, you may be well served by taking a multivitamin with minerals. This can help you get to a better nutritional state more quickly and will provide some of the essential vitamins and minerals that you may be lacking.

A pharmacist at any local drugstore should be able to recommend a good multivitamin plus minerals for you, and he or she can tell you if any of your medications need to be taken separately from the vitamin. Get a recommendation, get the vitamins, and take them as directed. Do this every day for the first thirty days.

Exercising During the First Thirty Days

Because of your previous alcohol use, you may have avoided physical exercise or exercised inconsistently. Once you stop drinking and begin to have some energy, you may feel inspired to get in shape physically and may want to initiate a training program or workout schedule of some kind right away. Although that idea is a positive one and a sure sign that you are on the right track, you should be aware that you have very little stamina at this point. Much of your energy will be used by the difficult task of abstaining from alcohol and learning your new lifestyle habits. Don't launch a boot-camp-style exercise schedule quite yet!

However, gradually beginning some physical activity at this time would be very helpful to you. Exercise can be a mood elevator and can help you feel better about yourself, which will decrease your chances of picking up a drink. Each day, try to spend some time doing simple stretches, walking, or some other form of exercise, such as yoga or swimming, that isn't overly taxing. If you want to get into serious workouts, give yourself a few weeks of adjustment time first.

12

Healthy Alternatives

BEVERAGE SELECTION can be a stumbling block for people as they quit drinking. Whether or not you know it, you probably have all sorts of attachments to the actual physical act of drinking. This might include the sound of a beer can opening, the act of pouring, the tinkling of ice, the feel of a bottle in your hand, the sensation of a beverage in your mouth, or swallowing.

What Do I Drink Now?

Many people with drinking problems continue to consume large numbers of beverages even after they have quit drinking alcohol. Because of this, it is important that you consider carefully what beverages you choose as part of your new lifestyle. Some choices will aid your efforts, and others may undermine them.

Reasons to Avoid Nonalcoholic Beer

Many brands of beer offer a nonalcoholic version. The truth is that these "nonalcoholic" beers do contain a small amount of alcohol. Granted, it is not a large amount, but if you consume enough of them in a row, you may experience some effect similar to an alcohol "buzz." Your goal is to stay away from alcohol entirely, so these beers are not a good choice for you.

The smell, taste, and look of nonalcoholic beer are designed to be as close as possible to actual beer. If you are drinking one, you'll notice that the difference between that beverage and a real beer isn't much. You will be reminded, through your senses of smell, taste, and sight, of the beer you are trying to leave behind. Your best bet is to switch to something completely different, something that doesn't have those associations for you.

Other Drinks to Avoid

Another thing to be wary of is switching to some type of beverage that has a noticeable mood-altering effect. For instance, if you drink a brand of pop—such as

Mountain Dew or Jolt—with high caffeine and sugar content, you'll feel some sort of "kick" from consuming it, especially if you consume it in large amounts. It's wise to avoid these kinds of beverages because they directly associate drinking something with altering your mood, precisely what you are trying to avoid.

Along those same lines, some beverages have recently been introduced that are specifically designed and advertised as stimulants. Stay away from these kinds of drinks as you are trying to achieve a steady balance in your physical body, which will help you maintain a steady balance in your mind—and help you avoid a return to alcohol. These "energy" drinks cause feelings of being revved up and might be followed by a feeling of being exhausted or let down. You want to learn to be in balance and to avoid getting your energy from a beverage.

Drink to Your Health

It is crucial that you stock up on an assortment of healthy beverages. You will find that you are thirsty, and if you don't have a supply of water or healthy beverages on hand, you may experience a craving. Buy several kinds of fruit juices in individual servings. Stock up on bottled water and explore some of the lightly flavored kinds, or make a pitcher of water with lemon or lime squeezed into it.

Buy milk, soy milk, or rice milk in individual cartons. Keep all of this chilled and within easy reach in your refrigerator. Separate the individual cartons or bottles from their wrappings so you can just reach in and grab one whenever you feel thirsty. Make things as easy as possible for yourself.

This is a good time in your life to try some beverages you may not have tried before. Consider making a trip to the health-food store or visit one online. You'll find a wide assortment of herbal teas, some of which make great-tasting iced tea, too. Many teas are rich in antioxidants, which may help undo some of the damage alcohol has done to your body.

Many unusual juices are available, such as pomegranate or blackberry, as well as some new mixtures of juice and tea. Try a variety of them, and when you discover which ones you like, stock up on them.

If you have a blender or can acquire one, buy ingredients for smoothies. Try different combinations of ingredients until you make a smoothie you really like. Ice, frozen fruit, yogurt, milk, orange juice, vanilla, and honey are all possibilities you could choose from as you learn to concoct the perfect smoothie.

Having a selection of healthy beverages in stock might seem like a silly thing, and if it were the only thing you were doing to try to quit drinking alcohol, you would almost surely fail. In combination with the rest of these suggestions, though, it can be a real help to you.

Switching Addictions

Because you have been relying on alcohol in a variety of ways, when you quit drinking there will be a noticeable emptiness in your daily life—it will definitely seem as if something is missing. The activity that used to relax you at the end of the day or keep you going during a long night is gone. One thing that is very likely to happen to you is that other mood-altering substances that you may already use—or have used in the past—will appeal to you even more.

Smoking Sober

Current or former tobacco users frequently increase their intake of tobacco—or take it up again—when they stop drinking. Many smokers or users of chewing tobacco will compensate for the lack of alcohol by focusing their attention on tobacco. They will light up or use some chewing tobacco in response to a craving for alcohol, in situations when they would have otherwise had a drink, or in reaction to some of the emotional discomfort they are experiencing as they quit drinking.

Some major drawbacks are associated with this technique. In addition to the dangers tobacco use can pose to the heart, lungs, throat, and the rest of the body, the increased use of tobacco causes the body to dehydrate, which can trigger more frequent or more intense cravings. The negative physical effects of tobacco use can also contribute to your feeling sluggish, wired, nervous, congested, or compromised. You do not have to quit smoking or chewing tobacco to quit drinking. It would make sense, however, to watch your tobacco use carefully and to make a commitment that you won't increase it as you get sober.

Other Addictive Drugs

People who quit drinking sometimes substitute mood-altering pain medications and prescription tranquilizers for alcohol. This is a dangerous practice, since many of those substances are addictive as well. If you end up alcohol-free but develop a dependence on pain pills instead, you haven't done yourself any favors. Also, those substances can weaken your resolve and contribute to poor decision making because they impair thinking.

If you have used marijuana or other street drugs in the past, you may be tempted to use them again. You might tell yourself that since you are no longer drinking, you deserve a little relaxation, something to take off the edge. If street drugs were never a problem for you in the past, you might not be able to see their danger to you now. Quitting drinking puts you in a vulnerable place to begin with, and you are at a higher risk of developing an addiction to these drugs. Just like the prescribed pain medications discussed earlier, marijuana, cocaine, and other street drugs impair your thinking and can easily lead to alcohol use because of this. Also, you have that new emptiness in your life because you have quit drinking. It would be all too easy to fill it up with another feel-good substance. Don't risk it. Make a commitment that you are going to learn to function without the aid of addictive, mood-altering drugs, prescription or otherwise.

In fact, it would be wise to think of yourself as a person who has become dependent on mood-altering chemicals—not "just" alcohol—even if alcohol is the primary substance you use. Long-term members of AA with many years of successful sobriety will tell you they cannot safely use any mood-altering substance. They don't smoke marijuana, and they only use prescription pain medication in situations where there are no alternatives. Even then, they adamantly request that the doctor supervise their use of the medication closely and not provide automatic refills.

You may think this is an overly cautious approach. In truth, it is based on many examples of problem drinkers who went on to demonstrate that they could not safely manage the use of any other mood-altering drug. Time after time, either they developed problematic use of the new substance or, while under the influence of something other than alcohol, they made a decision to return to drinking. Such decisions, made while judgment is clouded and their guard is down, are ones they often regret later. This caution about prescription drugs applies only to those types of drugs that are typically abused. Many prescription medications are vital and necessary for people to take, and you should not be concerned that these drugs, such as medication for high blood pressure or an antidepressant, will cause problems for your sobriety. Your doctor and pharmacist will know which medications are considered drugs of abuse, and they can provide guidance to you in this area.

Addictive Behaviors

The risk of switching addictions doesn't apply only to drugs. You might also find yourself drawn into repetitive behaviors that have some sort of sedating or mood-altering component to them. Examples of this include gambling, impulse shopping, viewing pornography, excessive sexual activity, or dangerous thrill seeking. Monitor yourself closely for these pitfalls in your sobriety. Avoid them if possible. If you become aware of any of these other addictions developing as you quit drinking, talk to somebody on your support list or attempt to stop by focusing on your positive sober activities.

If you cannot seem to control the new addictive behavior, it is time to get some professional help or join a self-help program like Gamblers Anonymous. If you are already involved in a substance-abuse treatment program, the staff there will be able to talk to you about this new addictive behavior and refer you, if necessary, to professionals who specialize in that area. If you have been getting sober without professional treatment and a new addiction has begun, please consider this a sign that you need some expert guidance.

How to Unwind Without a Drink

One of the most appealing and addictive qualities that alcohol has is the ability to relax a person quickly and efficiently. Dedicated drinkers come to rely on that almost instant relaxation, and over time they tend to forget how to relax in other ways. When they get sober, they suddenly feel very uptight, edgy, and high strung, and they don't have good tools for relieving that stressed-out feeling. This is a challenge during the early days and weeks of sobriety.

Keeping in mind that most Americans do not drink regularly, and they aren't all constantly uptight, there must be some other ways to relax besides the liquid variety. These alternatives to drinking are not quite so instantaneous as a quick shot of whiskey. In the long run, they are healthier and more sustainable techniques that don't interfere with your work, family relationships, or physical health. They will require some investment from you, in terms of time, practice, and in some cases money. But once you learn how to use these methods, they can serve you well for your lifetime.

Get a Massage

One of the fastest nonchemical routes to relaxation is massage. Massage therapists are experts at training your muscles to relax. They often employ the use of sound and aromatherapy, as well as manipulating your muscles and tissues, to help you release tension and feel calm and relaxed. These trained experts work with you to help you feel comfortable and at ease with the process. If you balk at the idea of a full-body massage, get an "executive" or "chair" massage that focuses on your back, shoulders, and neck.

Since the first few weeks of sobriety can be a tense time, consider scheduling a massage at least once, and even better once a week, during your first thirty days. Massage therapy gets better with time, as your therapist gets to know you and your muscles get trained to relax faster and more thoroughly each time. Find a massage therapist by asking your friends and family whom they might recommend, or go to the yellow pages of your phone book. If financial concerns are an issue, try calling the nearest massage therapy school and ask about getting free or low-cost massage therapy from students who are in their training program. Depending on where you live, you might also have access to other kinds of bodyworkers who are skilled in helping you relax and feel calm. Consider a skilled practitioner in reflexology, Reiki therapy, or biofeedback.

Meditate

Meditation or relaxation techniques are also important tools for you to learn about, practice, and develop as you quit drinking. Many people have stereotyped notions about meditation, picturing people sitting cross-legged with their palms upturned, chanting "ohm." While this picture is typical of one form of meditation, it is not the only way to meditate. Meditation involves training your mind to relax so that your body can deeply relax. It allows you to rest and regenerate at a very deep level, and over time it can increase your peacefulness and your ability to cope.

Often, people try to meditate without getting any education about it first. They usually find these early attempts to be frustrating, and they might decide as a result of one or two attempts that meditation doesn't work for them or is not something that they enjoy. People are not necessarily born knowing how to meditate successfully. Some basic training in meditation techniques will help it go much more smoothly.

Meditation tapes or CDs are readily available from bookstores, a variety of websites, or the library. They come in several forms. Some are simply composed of relaxing music or nature sounds. Others may include a person talking, who guides you through a particular relaxation technique or meditation practice. The speaker might be male or female, and he or she may focus on helping you relax your muscles, focus on your breathing, or center your thoughts. In "guided" meditations, the speaker may ask you to imagine yourself on some kind of journey or having a particular experience, such as picturing yourself walking on a beach. These are designed to help take you away from your everyday stress and to use your imagination to help you relax and restore yourself.

It is important to find a meditation tape or CD that you can listen to without feeling irritated. Some speakers' voices may have a quality that you dislike. Others may use chimes or wind sounds that are not soothing to you. At some book or music stores, you have the option to listen to a portion before purchasing, and this is recommended. Also, on some websites you may be able to hear a portion of the recording before purchasing it. This is also a good time to use your library so you can try out several options before selecting one for purchase.

Another possibility would be to ask the people on your support list if they have any that you could borrow.

One meditation CD on the market is specifically designed to help people with alcohol problems. It is titled "A Meditation to Support Your Recovery from Alcohol and Other Drugs" by Belleruth Naparstek and is published by Health Journeys. The speaker is a woman, and her voice is accompanied by a music score that was specifically designed for this meditation.

There is also a wide variety of books on meditation, including some that are very in-depth and others that are a short summary. *Meditation for Busy People* by Dawn Groves, for example, is a straightforward book that teaches you meditation techniques in the very first chapter. For a more comprehensive overview, try Stephen Levine's *A Gradual Awakening*.

In many cities, you can find meditation classes. Try bookstores, churches, healing arts centers, or massage therapy centers, or ask at the library. Often these are inexpensive or free, and they can be of great help to the beginner. Also, some therapists are specifically trained in relaxation techniques and can help you learn to relax as part of a therapy program.

If you belong to a church or synagogue or are involved in a faith community, seek out information about how to use prayer to relax. Like meditation, prayer can have a calming, soothing effect.

13

What You Need to Know About Sponsors

HOPEFULLY, BY this point in your sobriety, you are attending AA meetings regularly. You've no doubt heard the term *sponsorship* bandied about. It is a recommended part of the practices of AA that you get a sponsor. But what is a sponsor, exactly, and how can one be of help to you? How would you choose one? Once you have selected a potential sponsor, how do you go about getting that person to agree to sponsor you?

What Is a Sponsor?

A simple way to think about sponsors is that they are people who can guide new AA members through the pitfalls of early recovery because they have more experience in sobriety—usually, they have been sober for at least one year. A sponsor can help you get acquainted with other AA members, explain details about the practices and beliefs of AA, and guide you through the Twelve Steps that AA is based on. A relationship with a sponsor allows you to get straightforward advice and feedback from someone who cares about your sobriety but who is not at all involved in your personal life. In other words, sponsors can be objective because they aren't personally affected by your decisions. You might look at a sponsor as a kind of coach or advisor.

Some people are reluctant to get a sponsor because they feel they have enough people in their life already telling them what to do. With their employers, spouses, parents, this book, a probation officer, or a counselor, they feel overloaded with advice. Still, a sponsor can play a special role because he or she is well grounded in AA and has been down the road you are walking down. The unique kind of help a sponsor can provide can be a vital part of your sobriety.

One of the most important things to realize about sponsorship is that it helps the sponsor as much as it helps you. When AA was first being developed, one of the guiding principles was that alcoholics get sober by helping other alcoholics get sober. This was true back in the 1930s when the idea was first developed, and it still works today. People in AA are willing to be sponsors to newcomers because of how much it enriches and strengthens their own recovery. Keep this in mind if you worry about being a burden to a sponsor. You are giving your sponsor an opportunity to feel good about his or her own recovery, because he or she will be providing a valuable service to a new member. Almost everyone likes to feel needed.

How Do I Choose a Sponsor?

Keep in mind several factors as you begin observing people in AA for someone who might make a good sponsor for you. Number one, your sponsor should have good, solid sobriety. Someone who is struggling with his or her own recovery can't offer you much at this point.

It is standard practice that a person have at least a year of sobriety before serving as a sponsor. Some AA groups suggest your sponsor have at least three or four years of sobriety. In general, it is good to look for someone who has a significant amount of sobriety. Five or ten years would be great, but if you meet someone you really relate to and can talk easily with who has only eighteen months of sobriety, that might work out well, too.

How can you tell if the person you are considering as a potential sponsor has enough sobriety to be your sponsor? Often, people will mention their length of sobriety when talking in meetings. If that doesn't happen, you could ask the person directly. Approach your prospective sponsor after the meeting ends, and say something like, "I was impressed with some of the things you said in this meeting. Would you mind if I ask how long you have been sober?" Another approach is to ask someone else about your potential sponsor's length of sobriety. For instance, you could approach someone after the meeting and say, "I have been thinking about asking Joe to be my sponsor. Do you know how much sobriety he has?"

Second, you won't want your sponsorship relationship clouded by other distractions. Specifically, sexual attraction between an AA member and his or her sponsor can be disastrous because of the flirting and sly manipulations that may occur, even if they are unintentional. For this reason, it is strongly suggested that your sponsor be a member of your same sex. If you are gay or lesbian, this issue becomes a bit more complicated. In that case, you may want to consider having a sponsor of the opposite sex, keeping in mind that this may raise eyebrows in some conservative communities. If you are living in an urban area where AA meetings for gays and lesbians are available, ask at one of those meetings about the usual practices in your area regarding sponsorship and how best to avoid the potential conflict of finding yourself attracted to your sponsor.

Another important quality to look for in a sponsor is his or her level of involvement in the AA program. Your sponsor should be a person who regularly attends AA meetings and participates in AA functions such as dances, conferences, retreats, service work, or potluck dinners. This may seem like an obvious point, but often people try to choose someone as a sponsor who isn't even in AA, such as their uncle or a woman they know at work. If you know someone not in AA who quit drinking a long time ago, you can add them to your support list. But the role of a sponsor, in part, is to help you get comfortable attending AA meetings and functions. If that person isn't active in those activities, how can he or she help you?

Other Factors

Those three issues are the primary ones you should be concerned about when choosing a sponsor, but there are a few more things to consider.

Choose a sponsor you find friendly and approachable. If you are scared to talk to your sponsor because he or she is always gruff or distant, that person isn't a good choice for you. Alternatively, if someone seems too "touchy-feely" for you and you think you might fare better working with someone who is a little more stern and demanding, then that might be the best choice for you. Also, choose someone who has said something in a meeting that you found interesting or that you could relate to. You may want to look for someone who shares some similar background with you, but that is not required. Sometimes a sponsor from a very different background can work out just fine and can give you a completely different perspective on your life and your sobriety.

One more point about selecting sponsors: your relative or very close friend would not be the best person to be your sponsor. There may be things you won't feel comfortable sharing with that person. For the same reason, a person you are currently involved with romantically would not be a good sponsor, either. Keep the lines clean by choosing someone from outside of your immediate circle of family and friends.

Occasionally, newly sober people will say they don't need a sponsor because they have such a strong support network already. They might believe that their mother or girlfriend or best friend "won't let me drink even if I want to," and use this as reason for not getting a sponsor. The truth is, those people in your life can't keep you sober. If they could, they would have done so a long time ago. A sponsor can't ensure that you'll stay sober, either, but he or she has something to offer you that a loved one or relative cannot, and that is that your sponsor is currently succeeding at the very thing you want for yourself.

Also, it is acceptable to get a temporary sponsor. A temporary, or interim, sponsor is a contact person who agrees to provide support to you until you find someone who will work out on a longer-term basis. Sometimes, the temporary sponsor ends up becoming the actual sponsor, because you find that the arrangement works out well.

Some think they should attend AA for a while before they get a sponsor, but the truth is that you can get one right away. From your first AA meeting on, keep your eye out for someone who might fit the bill. It is never too early to get a sponsor, and the first few weeks of sobriety are an important time to have the extra help a sponsor can provide.

How Do I Go About Asking Someone?

There are several ways to get a sponsor. A method that leaves it somewhat up to chance involves announcing in an AA meeting that you are looking for a sponsor (or a temporary sponsor), and then saying, "If anyone is interested in being one, please talk to me after the meeting." Almost certainly, several people will approach you after the meeting and either offer to be a sponsor or offer their name and phone number as a person you can contact for support.

You may decide to be more selective. If you have been attending meetings and observing people for a potential sponsor, perhaps you have spotted one or more people who you think might be good candidates for you. If so, approach one of them immediately after an AA meeting and explain that you are new in AA and that you need to get a sponsor. You could say something like, "Do you sponsor people?" or you could plunge right in and say, "Would you be willing to sponsor me?" or "Would you be my interim sponsor?"

Most people are pleased to be asked, but that doesn't mean that your candidate will say yes to your request. Most likely he or she will accept, but there are several reasons why he or she might decline, including that the person doesn't have enough sobriety or is already sponsoring several people and doesn't feel he or she can give you the attention that you might need.

Try not to take it personally if you get turned down. Just keep looking around and asking people until you find one who agrees to be your sponsor. A person can sponsor more than one person at a time, so don't rule someone out as a potential sponsor just because you found out he or she is already sponsoring a few people.

Now What?

So, once you have a sponsor, what are you supposed to do next? Some people have the mistaken notion that your sponsor is someone you call when you feel like drinking.

But what if you don't feel like drinking anytime soon? What if several weeks go by and then you suddenly feel like drinking? By then your sponsor's phone number is tattered and torn, or lost, and you may question whether your sponsor would even remember you. Therefore, it is vital to build a connection with your sponsor before you get to the point where you need help resisting an urge to drink.

Some sponsors will tell you they want to hear from you at least once a day, just to check in and say how things are going. The beauty of this is that you get in the good habit of calling your sponsor when things are going well, so that when a crisis occurs, you feel comfortable dialing that number. If your sponsor doesn't suggest this, ask if it would be OK if you call several times a week at first. Your sponsor will almost certainly agree to that. Then, start doing it. At first, you may feel awkward about calling and wonder what to talk about. If you can manage to make the phone call and say who you are and that you are calling to check in, your sponsor will usually take it from there by asking you some questions—often ones not directly related to drinking. It is OK to just chat about your day. Phone calls with your sponsor don't have to be long and intense. The calls are a way to begin to build a comfortable familiarity between the two of you.

Other ways to build that connection include attending AA meetings together or meeting for lunch or a cup of coffee. These face-to-face meetings allow you to ask questions about AA, get support and advice regarding specific situations that are troubling you, or get your sponsor's thoughts on managing cravings. Feel free to ask for these kinds of connections.

Remember that your sponsor is just another AA member like you, but with more experience. Each sponsor will have his or her own personality and style of sponsoring. Many sponsors believe it is not their job to call the people they are sponsoring and won't ever do so. They will gladly be available for your phone calls, but they believe you need to show the initiative by reaching out. Ask your sponsor what he or she believes about this so you will know in advance whether you should expect him or her to call you.

Your sponsor is likely to have quite a few pieces of advice for you. You should listen carefully to what he or she tells you, since you did, after all, choose that person to be in a special position to offer you guidance. But like all of the advice and direction you get in AA, consider it to be suggestions. You are not forced, ordered, or required to do any of the things your sponsor tells you or anything the program tells you to do. They are all suggestions. Good, time-tested, well-considered suggestions, but suggestions nonetheless. You decide for yourself what ideas you will implement into your own life.

One good thing to keep in mind as you consider the suggestions made to you by your sponsor or other

AA members is that you have tried on your own before and eventually failed. It is possible that at this point in your life, with this particular problem, you might not know what is in your best interest. The first thought that comes into your head while trying to stay sober may not be the best one. These sober people are experts on staying sober. It might be smart to just do what they are doing, follow their guidance, and see if that doesn't work out well for you in the long run.

If It Doesn't Work Out

What if you end up with a sponsor who is not right for you? This happens sometimes. Maybe the person seemed like he or she would be a good match, but after a while you found out that he or she works the evening shift and you work during the day, so the person is never available in the evening when you need help most. Or perhaps your sponsor doesn't answer the phone or return your calls. Maybe the person does answer the phone, but he or she seems harried and rushed whenever you call. Are you stuck with this sponsor forever?

The answer is no. It is acceptable to change sponsors if the first one isn't working out for whatever reason. There is no need to assign blame or to end the relationship badly. You can just get another sponsor and then inform the first one that you have a new sponsor, and thank him or her for what he or she has done for you. Another option is to have more than one sponsor. That way, you could get a second sponsor and keep the first one, knowing the bulk of your support will come from the second one you have chosen. It is best, however, to be honest with both of your sponsors about what you are doing so that they know what to expect.

Be sure to add your sponsor's name and phone number to your support list. Also, for more in-depth information about sponsors, pick up the pamphlet "Questions and Answers About Sponsorship" at your AA meeting or at the central AA office in your community.

14

Restoring Your Spirit

The humiliation, fear, and helplessness associated with a serious drinking problem can feel like a massive weight on a person. Not only does the problem affect you physically and emotionally, but it also affects your spirit. Your spirit can be considered the part of you that harbors your beliefs, such as your sense of right and wrong. It is the part of you that feels a sense of justice or injustice. It is also felt by many to be the place where we store hope and our point of connection to something greater than ourselves. Alcohol addiction ravages spirits in many ways. It makes people feel as if they don't have any control over themselves and their behavior. It contributes to people going against their own value system in order to guard or disguise their drinking. Many people with drinking problems make and break numerous promises to themselves and to others. The end result is usually that the person with a drinking problem ends up feeling like a bad person.

Acknowledging a Damaged Spirit

In early sobriety, you may be acutely aware of your damaged spirit. Feeling regretful and ashamed of your actions and your current predicament are common. Many newly sober people wrestle with feelings that they have wasted their lives or that they didn't get sober soon enough. Because your thinking becomes clearer the further away you get from your last drink, you will be able to more fully understand the effect that your drinking, and its related behaviors, had on those around you. It often isn't a pretty picture. It is an easy time to be hard on yourself.

However, if you use this time to sharply criticize yourself for your past actions, you will have a more difficult time staying sober. The weight of your regrets can drag you right back to the bottle. Yes, you have done some things you wish you hadn't done. Yes, there are people you will need to apologize to about those actions. However, that cleanup time is not now.

The AA program provides a way for you to address the past actions you are feeling bad about. The eighth and ninth steps of the twelve-step program clearly spell out a system for addressing those you have wronged. Your sponsor and other AA members can provide you with support and guidance as you begin that process, which many people don't undergo until they have several months of sobriety under their belt. Your first thirty days is not the time for Steps Eight and Nine; it is not the time to address all the wrongs you have done or to beat yourself up over your current situation. Instead, this is the time for you to gain skills for sobriety, get through the initial withdrawal, build your support system, and learn how to manage the difficult task of staying alcohol-free. There will be time for making amends to those you have harmed, and those amends will be more believable if you have acquired some length of sobriety first.

Healing a Broken Spirit

As you make your way through the first thirty days of sobriety, your spirit will be working to restore itself. Beyond staying sober, you can assist in that restoration in several ways.

A Gratitude List

A simple tool that can help lift your spirit is writing a gratitude list. At the end of each day, write down one or more things that happened that day that you could be grateful for. Keep it simple. The list might include things like gratitude for being sober today, for the friendly clerk in the convenience store this morning, and for the fact that you were able to sleep last night. The items don't need to be profound or earth-shattering; in fact, the simpler they are, the better.

The act of making a daily gratitude list seems to send a message to your brain that you want to notice those types of things, and your awareness of pleasant aspects of your day will gradually increase. Although at first you might be having to really dream up something to put on the list, after doing it for some time you'll have many items to choose from each day. That doesn't mean that more good things are happening to you; it means your ability to notice them has improved.

A Simple Thank-You

Along those same lines, another practice you can try that will help you to restore your spirit is the simple act of thanking others. Your alcohol addiction has caused you to focus primarily on yourself and your own issues. In sobriety, you can begin to reach out to others more.

Thank people who do even small favors for you. Consider writing a thank-you note or e-mail to anyone who has helped you in a significant way lately. Maybe some of the people who are on your support list have been especially supportive. Call them or write to them to say how much you appreciate their help. Like a gratitude list, thanking others increases our awareness of how much others do for us each day.

Getting Back in Touch with God

If you have had a set of religious or spiritual beliefs in the past, consider revisiting them. You may find that you drifted away from those beliefs because of your focus on your alcohol use or because of guilt associated with your drinking. Now that you are starting to get sober, you may feel drawn to beliefs and practices that once mattered to you. Examples of ways to reconnect might include attending a worship service or beginning to pray again.

If you find you have conflicted feelings about any of your spiritual or religious beliefs, which is not uncommon during this time when you are reevaluating your life, you could talk with your sponsor or a clergy member about those conflicts. Many people who once believed in a traditional concept of God find themselves angry or alienated because they asked for help with their drinking problem and feel as though the help didn't come. Talking this over with an understanding person may help you sort it out.

That process of sorting out what you believe is not a quick one. Throughout your recovery you will have opportunities to explore your values and beliefs, and as long as alcohol isn't clouding your mind, you should feel better equipped to deal with those types of questions in your life. You don't need to get that issue settled during your first month of sobriety—give yourself a little breathing room.

The Power of Reflection

Reconnecting with your spirit can also be done through art, music, or spending time in nature. The simple act of watching the sun go down, walking through a garden or an art gallery, or listening to music that inspires you can help you find a sense of hope. Avoid music that reminds you of your drinking days. Consider buying or borrowing some music that is new to you, and think of it as your sobriety music. If you have enjoyed artistic activities in the past, see if they interest you now. Read or write a poem, sketch something in your notebook, dig a set of paints out of a back closet, or even simply buy a coloring book with some crayons. For some people, these kinds of creative actions can be soothing and are reminders of the small, sober pleasures that are still available. Remember not to take on too large of a project at this early stage of your recovery. You can't write the great American novel or paint a masterpiece while you are struggling to stay sober each day. Save those accomplishments for a little later in your recovery.

By staying sober, you are allowing yourself to regain your dignity. Each day you are likely to feel less ashamed and more hopeful. Watch for those signs of your spirit lifting, such as a renewed sense of hope or a return of your sense of humor. The changes will be gradual, but as long as you are not drinking, you can trust that they will happen.

15

Notes About Failure

THERE ARE those who will read this book, try the suggestions, and still find themselves unable to quit drinking. This section is specifically for those people. This is not the time to give up on yourself, even though you may feel like doing so. You may be wondering why others can successfully get sober but you cannot. You may suspect there is something flawed about you that will prevent you from ever getting your life together. This is not the case, and there is still hope for you. Some people simply have a harder time with this than others. Many factors can contribute to the difficulty. Not having enough support, being afraid or unwilling to engage in AA, or an underlying problem such as depression or anxiety can make recovery especially stressful.

Getting Sober Is Not Easy

The simple fact is that getting sober is not easy. Some people fail when they first attempt it. Some fail even after several tries. The good news is that even people who have failed before can eventually get sober, and stay sober, for the rest of their lives.

Many long-timers in AA will tell you they went to treatment three or four times before they finally "got it." There are many examples of people who attempted sobriety, with the help of professional treatment, eight or ten times before they eventually succeeded. This may seem discouraging to you and may make you feel as though you will have to suffer through many attempts before you get it right. Instead, let it be inspiring to you. The underlying message is that there are no hopeless cases. If you are breathing, there is hope for you.

Trying Again

If you have tried and failed, you have the benefit of knowing what worked and what didn't work for you. This will help you as you get back on the wagon. The information is especially relevant because it played itself out in your own life with your particular set of circumstances.

Neglected Areas of Recovery

Pay particular attention to the events that led you back to drinking. Were you spending time with friends who still drink? Did you have a "tornado trigger" and try to tough it out without increasing your support? Go back through the sections of this book and identify any areas where you decided the advice didn't apply to you or seemed too difficult to actually do. These areas may have new meaning for you now.

It is important to look at the level of support you arranged for yourself and to find ways to increase that support. For instance, if you tried to get sober without any AA involvement, you'll need to reconsider that position now. If you did go to AA but decided against any professional treatment options, now might be a good time to access treatment. What you were doing during your attempt to get sober wasn't quite enough for you. To increase your chance of success with your new attempt, you will have to increase your involvement in your recovery.

But I Did Everything Right!

What if you are one of those people who actually did everything "by the book" and still failed? Let's say you stayed away from any contact with alcohol, got involved in AA, called your sponsor, went to treatment and followed their suggestions, tried meditation, ate healthy foods, got sufficient rest, drank extra water, and still ended up drinking. Likely you are feeling pretty disappointed at this time.

Is Medication Right for You?

Occasionally, special medical issues complicate a person's ability to get and stay sober. If you can honestly tell yourself that you have "tried everything" and still can't avoid drinking, it is time to take a deeper look at your situation. Here are some options.

If extreme cravings are making it impossible for you to stay away from drinking, consider talking to your doctor about medications such as Revia (naltrexone) or Campral (acamprosate calcium). These drugs are approved by the FDA to treat alcoholism. Though they each have different effects within the body, both Revia and Campral appear to reduce cravings, decrease your desire for alcohol, and increase the likelihood that you will remain alcohol-free. These are not mood-altering drugs, and people do not become dependent on them. Although some side effects are associated with them, they are usually mild and short-lived. Most people tolerate these medicines well. As with all medication, some people should not take them, such as pregnant women and anyone with severe liver damage. Your doctor can help decide whether either one is an appropriate medication for you, and if so, it might be just the thing you need to help you into sobriety. Keep in mind, though, that medication is not a substitute for all the other work that sobriety requires.

Living Situation

One of the main culprits that contributes to continued drinking is living in a situation that doesn't support sobriety. If this is your situation, it is time for you to take a serious look at your alternatives. A residential treatment program, a halfway house (where you live under supervision with other people in recovery and have to abide by curfews and random substance-abuse testing), or a sober living house (such as an Oxford House, where the rules of the house are enforced by the people living there) might be necessary for you to succeed with your goal of being sober. You may have resisted taking this step before. Consider it now. Although it may seem like a scary proposition, it could well save your life.

Addressing Mental Health Disorders

Mental health disorders such as anxiety and depression can make it especially challenging for people to get sober. Look into a psychological evaluation, which might involve some written testing as well as an interview. A licensed psychologist will use this testing to offer you insight into any mental health conditions or tendencies that may be barriers to your sobriety. The testing will result in some recommendations, which may include psychotherapy to address unresolved issues or overcome long-standing patterns that are dragging you down. The psychologist might also suggest that you could benefit from medication to treat a mental health disorder, and he or she will be able to refer you to a physician who can prescribe the medication for you.

Another alternative is to be assessed by a psychiatrist, a physician who specializes in the diagnosis and treatment of mental illness. Most doctors or clinics can refer you to a psychiatrist. The psychiatrist may recommend medication for you; if this happens, be sure to ask whether the medications are considered mood-altering or are of any danger to someone with an alcohol problem. Antidepressants are generally considered safe for use by people in recovery.

The Role of Family

Another factor in people's success is whether their family members and close friends are involved in their recovery. If you are going to AA, get some materials for your family members about Al-Anon, and ask them if they would support you by attending some meetings. Al-Anon will help them learn how to be supportive of your recovery and how to stop doing things they don't mean to do that may encourage you to continue drinking.

If you are involved in a professional treatment program or plan to be, be sure to find out how your family members and closest friends can be included. Look into classes, support groups, or family counseling that may be a part of the treatment package.

Of course, you should not take this as an opportunity to blame your family for your return to drinking. Their support can increase your chances of success, but ultimately, your recovery is your own responsibility. People can and do get sober with no support at all within their own family.

Can You Surrender?

In AA, you will sometimes hear people talk about whether or not they have surrendered. This refers to the tendency that many people have to do things their own way. You might realize you have a problem, for example, but because of your pride, or a stubborn streak, or just plain defiance, you don't want to "give in" and do the things that are suggested in order to get sober. You may feel you're not like "them," that you're different and can do it your way.

This attitude puts you in a particularly uncomfortable spot. You know you want to stop drinking, you have tried and failed, but you just don't want to give yourself entirely to this new life that sobriety would require. When people surrender to their sober lives, and all of the changes that go along with it, they are amazed at how much easier sobriety gets. Before that point, they were wrestling with their drinking problem while wrestling with themselves at the same time. No wonder they failed. It wasn't a fair fight.

This may be a good time to reflect on your own level of commitment to your sobriety. Have you really taken all of the steps that you could have? Are there certain ways you have tried to go against the flow, by doing things your own way, and by doing so put your sobriety in danger? Maybe it is time to stop fighting against the changes and try a new way. Learn from the experience of the millions of sober people who are living new lives filled with meaning and purpose. If doing things your way isn't working, maybe it is time to wave the white flag and say, "I give up." By doing so, you become willing to do whatever it takes to get sober.

For many stubborn cases, surrender is the doorway to sobriety. Keep trying. Do whatever you need to do to keep staking a claim on your new life. If you are already doing all the things that have been advised to you, do more of them. Ask your sponsor for more help, get a second sponsor, see your doctor, confide in your pastor, priest, or rabbi, or ask for more treatment. Use your resourcefulness to continue to seek answers until you have them. Remember, there is no such thing as a hopeless case.

During AA meetings, there is often a pause for a moment of silence for the people who are "still suffering." This moment of silence, which many use as a moment of prayer, is repeated countless times per day, in cities and towns all over the world. If you are still drinking in spite of your best efforts, know that millions of people each day are holding you in their thoughts or prayers. Let this be an encouragement to you as you find your way back to sobriety.

Afterword: Seeing Beyond Thirty Days

THIRTY DAYS of sobriety is a huge accomplishment for people who previously worried they couldn't even stay sober for a week or two. AA members the world over celebrate thirty days of sobriety by awarding a "thirty-day coin," also called a chip or medallion. It is a significant benchmark on your way into long-term sobriety. If you have become involved in AA during the past thirty days, ask your sponsor or another AA member about how you can get a thirty-day medallion. Most meetings keep a supply of them, or your sponsor might be the one to present it to you.

What Do Sober People Do for Fun?

One of the most difficult aspects of being newly sober is the feeling that any chance of having fun has gone out of your life. When you think back about enjoyable times you had in the past, you probably recall times when you were drinking. Most of your activities likely revolved around alcohol or took place in settings where alcohol is readily available. Now that you don't drink, your future might look boring, drab, flat, and lifeless.

In the early days and weeks of your sobriety, you might feel as though you have lost the ability to have fun. Your stress level is elevated, you may find it hard to relax, and you may be dealing with an increase in irritability. You will have pulled back from all of your drinking buddies and habits, so you can no longer go out to let off some steam playing pool at the bar or hanging out with the girls over a few drinks. You may be afraid to do much of anything for fear that you'll run into a trigger or forget yourself and make a beeline for your favorite liquor store. Even if you go out and do some fun, sober things, you might not be a person who can really enjoy those things—yet. Does this mean you must resign yourself to a dull and boring life in order to stay sober?

Actually, you will find it is just the opposite. Eventually, you will become very talented at recognizing the fun in a wide variety of activities and will enjoy many things that you never would have gotten around to doing if you were still drinking. You might rediscover your creativity, and old interests that you may have forgotten about will resurface. It will take some time, however.

When alcohol-related activities are your main source of fun, you can slowly lose your creativity concerning your recreational outlets. Planning enjoyable activities takes a certain amount of energy and focus, and much of your energy and focus has been directed toward the maintenance of your drinking habit. Also, the euphoria-inducing properties of alcohol can make certain things seem fun at the time, even if they are activities you wouldn't normally enjoy with people you actually don't like.

Sober Fun

You can do several things while you are waiting for your "fun meter" to repair itself. First of all, begin trying out different recreational activities. Start small, since so much of your energy will be going toward just getting through the day sober. Now is not the time to take up yachting or to learn a complicated game like chess for the first time. If those things interest you, take them up a little later in your sobriety. Instead, try some small-scale leisure activities, such as playing a card game you already know how to play or walking the trails in the nature center that you are already familiar with.

As you go through these first weeks of staying sober, pay special attention to any old interests that you find are resurfacing. Perhaps you used to sew and now you are thinking about digging your boxes of fabric out of the back closet. Maybe you used to enjoy bike riding and you need to get a bike tire repaired. These kinds of activities are great to rediscover now, because they don't require you to learn new information at a time when your brain is preoccupied. Also, you already know that you enjoy them, or at least that you once enjoyed them. Write these returning interests down in your notebook, and feel free to take the small steps required to reinvolve yourself in these pursuits.

As you are reading or watching television, jot down any activities that the characters are doing that sound even remotely interesting, even if you have no idea how you would ever do such an activity yourself. Later, you might find yourself in a situation where you can explore these interests further.

How to have fun as a sober person is a great topic of conversation to discuss with your sponsor or other AA members. Remember, you can hang around after an AA meeting and chat informally, and that would be a good time to say something as simple as "Did you guys find it hard to have fun when you were first sober?" or maybe "What kinds of things do you do for fun now that you don't drink?" As silly as it seems, you probably have forgotten how to have fun without alcohol, and people who have been through it will know exactly what you are talking about and exactly how you are feeling.

Trying Something New

Be open to new experiences, especially if you are being invited by a sober friend. If a group from your AA meeting has a plan to go fishing together and you have never been interested in fishing, consider trying it anyway. If they are going to meet up with one another to race go-carts at a local track, think about joining them. Whatever they are doing, it will likely be a better option than sitting home alone trying not to drink. By experiencing new activities, you may run across one or more that you really like, which will help you learn to have fun without drinking.

On a cautionary note, beware of the burst of energy you may get in early sobriety. You may have a day, or even several days in a row, during which you feel so much better than you had been feeling, and a new strength and feeling of vitality comes over you. This is a wonderful sensation, and you will enjoy it if it happens to you. But don't mistake it for your new way of being, as it might be temporary. It could last for a day, or even a week, but it is likely that you will have more times of feeling down, stressed, or lacking in energy. The road to sobriety is long and sometimes difficult, so although it's important to enjoy these little bursts of energy, don't mistake them for a new reality.

Therefore, you might not want to "take on the world" when those energy bursts come. People in very early sobriety have gone out and invested in expensive sports equipment or signed up for strenuous classes at the local gym, but the following week they were disappointed in themselves for not following through. Or they tried to force themselves to do the activity because they had paid for it, even if the enthusiasm was long gone. If you get an energy burst, be glad for it, but don't overdo it and don't assume you'll always feel that great.

Over time, you will discover that people who don't drink enjoy a wide, exciting variety of activities in their free time. Whether stargazing or scuba diving, writing novels or acting in plays, arrowhead hunting or making quilts, white water rafting or raising dogs, sober people pursue their leisure interests with energy, focus, and enthusiasm. Soon, you will be doing so as well. Eventually, instead of wondering what sober people do for fun, your life may be filled with so many opportunities that you'll wonder how you ever had time to drink.

Identifying Sober Friends

Once you have been sober for thirty days, you are getting closer to being able to identify which of your friends are friends and which were actually drinking buddies. If you have been clear with your friends about your plan to get sober and you have not spent time in places where drinking is happening, then you probably have an idea already about who the drinking buddies were. They may have expressed support to you in the beginning, but over the past thirty days you may have heard from them less and less. Some of your drinking buddies simply couldn't seem to understand what you were setting out to do with this plan to get sober. They still called and invited you to the bar or to parties, or they showed up at your door with alcohol in hand. These are people who are so involved in the drinking culture that they can't really be supportive to you.

Does it mean that he or she wasn't really your friend? That is not particularly important to figure out right now. Maybe you had a legitimate friendship with this person, or maybe your time together mostly revolved around alcohol. Either way, if this person can't grasp your need to be alcohol-free and your plan to physically stay away from drinking environments, then this person can't be a good friend to you now. His or her lack of support could sabotage the better life you are working toward for yourself.

Some of your other friendships might not be so clear. You may have friends who verbally support you and don't encourage you to drink, but their own lives are so closely linked to alcohol that the friendship presents problems now that you are sober. What does the future hold for these friendships? Some of these people might, over time, learn how to spend time with you that doesn't involve drinking. These might be friends you occasionally go to breakfast with, for instance. However, if their conversation is focused on how much fun they had at a party last night, how many tequila shots so-and-so took last week at the bar, or other drinking stories, you will find that you don't enjoy their company much anymore—and they might not enjoy yours anymore, either.

Probably you have a friend or two whom you drank with in the past who is not dedicated to drinking and can easily make the transition to being your friend when you are sober. Some of these people will welcome the positive change in you and may feel more comfortable with you as a friend now that you aren't so unpredictable. This kind of friendship may actually deepen as a result of your sobriety, and you will value these friends more than you did before.

AA After Thirty Days

If you have been attending AA meetings regularly in the past thirty days, you have become accustomed to their way of doing things. The language they use probably doesn't seem so foreign to you anymore, and if you have consistently gone to the same meetings, the faces are becoming familiar. You may know many of their first names by now.

What does your future in AA look like? If you continue your regular involvement, you will discover many people who share common interests with you. You will come to enjoy your AA friends for their stories, their sense of humor, their wisdom, or their ability to have a wild, fun time without drinking. If you are talking at least a little bit in the meetings and you don't race out of there right after the prayer, you'll eventually be invited to social gatherings, such as football parties, campouts, softball games, weekend retreats at a state park, or potluck dinners. You'll exchange phone numbers and build friendships with many sober people.

One day, you will be in an AA meeting and a brand-new person will come in for the first time. He or she might seem scared or tearful. He or she might pass up the opportunity to talk during the meeting. Afterward, you find yourself eager to talk with this newcomer and to offer a little encouragement. You will be able to see yourself in this scared first-timer. Then, you'll realize that you are no longer a newcomer yourself. You are comfortable enough to reach out to another person. This is an important turning point in your sobriety, when you realize you have something to offer to someone else.

Eventually, after at least a year in sobriety, when you've learned about the Twelve Steps and built your AA community of friends, someone might ask you to be a sponsor. Today, that may seem far-fetched, but keep in mind that all these AA experts, who talk knowledgeably about the program and sponsor other people, were people just like you at one time. They had their first AA experience, they were nervous or uncomfortable, and they once knew nothing about how to stop drinking. What makes them know so much now? They have learned from their own experience in sobriety and their regular attendance at AA meetings. This can happen to you, as well.

Reconciling with Your Past

In early sobriety, you may feel as though the damage you have caused to relationships cannot be repaired. Perhaps you have destroyed a career, or a marriage, or your relationship with your parents. Although it is a sad fact that some damage cannot ever be healed—and it would be pointless to pretend otherwise—the truth is that a great deal of damage *can* be resolved over time. Maybe you will never get your ex-wife, ex-girlfriend, ex-husband, or ex-boyfriend to take you back. However, if you remain sober and continue to work on your issues through the help of a sponsor, AA friends, a counselor, or a treatment program, you will certainly have the chance of having healthy, fulfilling relationships in the future. You may be amazed at how close and intimate those relationships can be, with your newfound knowledge of yourself and without the screen of alcohol keeping you apart.

Families are often eager to forgive your past and have a new bond with you. If your family seems reluctant, it is probably because of how much your drinking and the behavior that went with it has hurt them. If you stay sober, they will likely be watching, and over time they will regain some trust in you. You may want their trust right away, but it always takes time to rebuild it. It took you a long time to inflict the damage to your family relationships—don't expect it to be resolved overnight.

One possibility is that as you stay sober and get more emotionally healthy, you may see your family in a new light. Their own patterns of dealing with issues or feelings may now seem unhealthy to you, and you may be especially sensitive to the ways they avoid, defend, or deny problems.

You can learn about yourself through these observations, but your first year of sobriety is probably not the best time to start pointing out what is wrong with them. Remember, your drinking has probably been a big part of the trouble in your family. This would be a good time to pay close attention to yourself, your own problems, and your own recovery and not dwell too much on the problems of others.

It may be that you will discover the need to make some changes in the way that you communicate with your family as you pursue your sobriety. It would be a good idea to work closely with your sponsor or a counselor to make sure you go about this in a direct and healthy manner. Sometimes, stored feelings can come out all at once, making others feel dumped on or overwhelmed. Your family shouldn't have to suffer needlessly because of your new sobriety. This isn't a time to take things out on them. Seek good guidance on these issues so you don't end up saying things that you regret.

If you have children, it is likely that they will be among the first to restore their relationship with you. Be sure to avoid making promises to them, either about your ongoing sobriety or about ways you plan to make things up to them. Not only do actions speak louder than words, but they are also the only way real healing takes place. Each day, do what you need to do to stay sober, then do what you can to restore your relationship with them, and let time take care of the rest.

It is suggested that people in their first year of sobriety should not make any life-altering decisions, such as getting married or divorced. The reason for this is that your life is changing rapidly during this first year, and situations that look wonderful, or intolerable, might look very different a year from now.

The Future Looks Bright

You can expect to continue to improve physically over the course of your sobriety. You will notice that you have more energy, can think clearly, and look better overall. The empty calories of alcohol have been replaced with healthier options, and this will show up in your overall appearance.

If you didn't switch addictions into something like gambling or compulsive spending, your finances will start to stabilize in recovery. You are more able to work consistently, and your performance at work will be better. You aren't spending money on alcohol, which will likely be quite a savings for you. You may be paying off debt from your previous lifestyle, but you should notice progress in this area as your sobriety continues.

Embedded in the AA literature are many positive statements about what you can expect in the future. The ones most often referred to follow the information about Step Nine in the book titled *Alcoholics Anonymous*, nicknamed the Big Book, and are called "The Promises." Look them up and be encouraged by them. Other positive declarations are found in the recovery literature, and you can read them with the knowledge that they are based on the experiences of many people and can come true for you, too. One of these statements from the Big Book is, *"In the face of collapse and despair, in the face of the total failure of their human resources, they found that a new power, peace, happiness, and sense of direction flowed into them."* Many people with long-term sobriety will tell you this is true for them, and it is my sincere hope that this will be true for you.

You will not spend the rest of your sober days feeling as though you are missing out on the fun of drinking. Your new life will become so enriching, so full of new companions and activities, that you will be grateful for your sobriety. The cravings you may experience in the early days of your sobriety will lessen over time. Your old life, if it still held any appeal for you, will no longer have anything to offer you. You will be uplifted by your new sense of self-worth, your connections to others, and your sense of well-being. You will want to do the things necessary to preserve your sobriety because of how much you value the way you feel. Taking care of your sobriety will not seem like a chore, but a new and remarkable way of life.

Index

AA Grapevine Online, 69–70
AA History and Trivia site, 70
Addictions
  drugs, 116–18
  tobacco, 115–16
Addictive behaviors, 118–19
Al-Anon, 150
Alcohol
  Banned-from-My-Hand rule for, 59–62
  cravings, 55–58
  expensive collections of, 12–13
  healthy alternatives to, 113–15
  religious traditions and, 62–64
  unwinding without, 119–23
Alcoholics Anonymous (AA)
  benefits from, 49–50
  Big Book, 46, 52, 167
  defined, 37
  founders of, 84
  introductions at, 48–49
  meetings, 41–48
  reasons for resisting, 37–41
  as safety net, 36
  surrender, 151–53
Alcoholics Anonymous (AA) after thirty days, 162–64

Antidepressants, 150
Anxiety, 149

Banned-from-My-Hand rule, 59–62
Beer, nonalcoholic, 112
Beverages, healthy, 113–15
Beverages to avoid, 112–13
Big Book, 46, 52, 84, 167
Bob, Dr., 84
Boredom, 82–85

Caffeine, 106
Campral (acamprosate calcium), 148
Casey, Karen, 85
Chewing tobacco, 115–16
Clean and Sober, 84
Clearing a space
  clearing physical space, 10–12
  expensive collections and, 12–13
  living with someone who drinks, 13–15
  where you like to drink, 15–16
Cocaine, 117
Coffee, 106
Communion wine, 63
Cravings, 55–58
Crying, 77–78

Daily meditations, 85
Decision to get sober, 53–55
Depression, 149
Detox, 24
Drinking buddy, 3–4
Drinking triggers
  during first thirty days, 96–98
  living with, 102–3
  other behaviors and, 96
  personal, 100–102
  termite, 89–96
  tornado, 88–89, 147
  trigger locks, 98–100
Drinks, healthy, 113–15
Drinks to avoid, 112–13
Drugs, addictive, 116–18

Each Day a New Beginning, 85
Eating, 108–9
Eisenberg, Arlene, 84
Eisenberg, Howard, 84
Emotions
  boredom, 82–85
  dealing with, 76–77
  duration of moodiness, 75–76
  grief, 80–82
  letting it out, 77–78
  making up for lost time, 85–86

suppression of, 74–75
writing it down, 78–80
Exercise, 106, 110

Failure or success
factors in, 145
family's role and, 150–51
inspiring message about, 146
living situation and, 149
medication and, 148–49
mental health disorders and, 149–50
neglected areas of recovery and, 147
surrender and, 151–53
Family, role of, 150–51
Feelings
boredom, 82–85
dealing with, 76–77
duration of moodiness, 75–76
grief, 80–82
letting it out, 77–78
making up for lost time, 85–86
suppression of, 74–75
writing it down, 78–80
Films, 83–84
Friends, sober, 160–62
Fruit juices, 113
Fun for sober people, 156–60
Future, your, 167–68

Gambling, 118, 119, 167
God, getting in touch with, 141–42
Gratitude list, 139–40
Grief, 80–82
Groves, Dawn, 123

Healing broken spirit
getting in touch with God, 141–42
gratitude list, 139–40
reflection, 142–43
thanking others, 140–41
Health insurance, 31–33, 35–36

Insurance, health, 31–33, 35–36
Internet
online limitations, 70–71
power of, 65–67
searches, 67–68
useful sites, 68–70

Kidman, Nicole, 70

Levine, Stephen, 123
Living situation, 149
Living Sober, 85

Marijuana, 116–17
Massage, 120–21
Meals, 108–9
Medical assistance for withdrawal, 19–22
Medication
  prescription, 117–18
  for treatment of alcoholism, 148–49
Meditation, 121–23
Meditations, daily, 85
Mental health disorders, 149–50
Mooney, Al J., 84
Movies, 83–84
My Name is Bill W, 84

Naparstek, Belleruth, 123
Nonalcoholic beer, 112

Online help
  Internet searches, 67–68
  limitations of, 70–71
  power of Internet, 65–67
  useful sites, 68–70
Oxford House, 149

Past, reconciling with, 164–66
Personal triggers, 100–102
Physical activity, 106, 110
Pop, 112–13
Prescription medications, 117–18
Professional treatment
  cost of, 31–36
  myths about, 23, 25
  options, 25–31
  terminology, 24

The Recovery Book, 84
Reflection, 142–43
Regrets, 138
Rehab, 24
Relaxing without a drink
  massage, 120–21
  meditation, 121–23
  other ways to relax, 119–20
Religion
  Alcoholics Anonymous and, 39–41, 45–46
  getting in touch with God, 141–42
Religious traditions and alcohol, 62–64
Residential treatment, 27–30, 149
Revia (naltrexone), 148

Serenity Prayer, 46, 70, 99
Sleep
- caffeine and, 106
- disturbed, 107–8
- exercise and, 106
- importance of, 105
- sounds and, 106–7

Sleeping aids, chemical, 107
Smoking, 115–16
Sober friends, 160–62
Sober fun, 156–60
Sober24.com, 68–69
Soda pop, 112–13
Spirit
- damaged, 138–39
- defined, 137
- healing broken, 139–43

Spohn, David, 85
Sponsor
- advice from, 134–35
- asking someone, 131–32
- choosing, 127–31
- connecting with, 132–34
- defined, 126–27
- temporary, 131

Stimulants, 113
Substance Abuse & Mental Health Services Administration (SAMHSA), 34
Success or failure
- factors in, 145
- family's role in, 150–51
- inspiring message, 146
- living situation and, 149
- medication and, 148–49
- mental health disorders and, 149–50
- neglected areas of recovery and, 147

Supplies, 1–2, 51–52
Support
- enlisting, 6–8
- list, 4–6

Surrender, 151–53

Terminology, treatment, 24
Thanking others, 140–41
Thirty-day medallion, 155
Tobacco use, 115–16
Treatment, professional
- cost of, 31–36
- myths about, 23, 25
- options, 25–31
- terminology, 24

Triggers
- during first thirty days, 96–98
- living with, 102–3
- other behaviors and, 96

personal, 100–102
termite, 89–96
tornado, 88–89, 147
trigger locks, 98–100
28 Days, 84
Twenty-Four Hours a Day, 85

Unwinding without a drink
massage, 120–21
meditation, 121–23
other ways to relax, 119–20

Websites, useful, 68–70
When a Man Loves a Woman, 84
Williams, JoBeth, 84
Wilson, Bill, 84
Wilson, Lois, 84
Withdrawal
defined, 17–18
life-threatening nature of, 18–19
medical assistance for, 19–22
Woods, James, 84